Quest 1

Teacher's Edition

 **Reading and Writing**

Student Book Authors
Pamela Hartmann
Laurie Blass

Teacher's Edition Writer
Kristin Sherman

 **McGraw-Hill**

Quest 1 Reading and Writing Teacher's Edition

Published by McGraw-Hill ESL/ELT, a business unit of The McGraw-Hill Companies, Inc., 1221 Avenue of the Americas, New York, NY 10020.

ISBN13: 978-0-07-326577-3
ISBN10: 0-07-326577-2
1 2 3 4 5 6 7 8 9 QPD/QPD 12 11 10 09 08 07 06

Editorial director: Erik Gundersen
Series editor: Linda O'Roke
Development editor: Christina Schafermeyer
Production manager: Juanita Thompson
Production coordinator: MaryRose Malley
Cover designer: David Averbach, Anthology
Interior designer: Karolyn Wehner

McGraw-Hill

www.esl-elt.mcgraw-hill.com

The **McGraw·Hill** Companies

TABLE OF CONTENTS

●●●●● WELCOME To The Teacher's Edition

The *Quest* Teacher's Edition provides support and flexibility to teachers using the *Quest* Student Book. Each chapter of the Teacher's Edition begins with a chapter overview that includes a brief summary of the Student Book chapter, a list of the vocabulary words found in the chapter, a list of the reading, critical thinking, and writing strategies highlighted throughout the chapter, as well as a list of the mechanics presented and practiced in that chapter. In addition, the Teacher's Edition provides step-by-step teaching procedures; notes on culture, grammar, vocabulary, and pronunciation; expansion activities; photocopiable masters of select expansion activities; Internet research ideas; answer keys; and end-of-chapter tests.

Procedures

❍ Experienced teachers can use the step-by-step procedural notes as quick guides and refreshers before class, while newer or substitute teachers can use the notes as a more extensive guide in the classroom. These notes also help teachers provide context for the activities and assess comprehension of the material covered.

Answer Keys

❍ Answer keys are provided for all activities that have definite answers. In cases where multiple answers could be correct, possible answers are included. Answer keys are also provided for the Vocabulary Workshop after each unit.

Notes

❍ Where appropriate, academic culture, grammar, vocabulary, and pronunciation notes provide background information, answers to questions students might raise, or points teachers might want to review or introduce. For example, in *Quest 1 Reading and Writing* Chapter 1, a reading refers to Ben & Jerry's ice cream, so a cultural note provides some background information on the ice cream company. These notes are provided at the logical point of use, but teachers can decide if and when to use the information in class.

TOEFL® iBT Tips

❍ In each chapter, six tips for the TOEFL® iBT are given with corresponding notes on how strategies and activities from the student book chapter can help students practice and prepare for the exam. Examples of TOEFL® iBT question format are also given in these tips.

Expansion Activities

❍ At least 10 optional expansion activities are included in each chapter. These activities offer teachers creative ideas for reinforcing the chapter content while appealing to different learning styles. Activities include games, conversation practice, and working with manipulatives such as sentence strips, projects, and presentations. These expansion activities often allow students to practice all four language skills, not just the two skills that the student book focuses on.

Photocopiable Masters

○ Up to three master worksheets that teachers can photocopy are included for each chapter. These worksheets are optional and are described in expansion activities located within the chapter. One chapter worksheet is often additional editing practice, while the others might be a graphic organizer or a set of sentence strips.

End-of-Chapter Tests

○ The end-of-chapter tests assess students on reading comprehension, one or more of the reading or critical thinking strategies highlighted in the chapter, vocabulary, mechanics, and editing. Item types include multiple choice, fill-in-the-blank, and true/false, for a total of 35 items per test. Answer keys are provided.

Website Research

○ At the end of Part 3 in each chapter of the Teacher's Edition, a list of suggested website resources provides additional information on the topics presented in the chapter. Teachers may use this optional resource to gather more background or to direct students to these sites to research the topics for an expansion activity.

Scope and Sequence

Chapter	Reading Strategies	Writing Strategies
Getting Started • Introduction: *Getting the Most out of a Textbook*	• Guessing the Meaning from Context • Keeping a Word Journal • Understanding Parts of Speech • Understanding Parts of Speech: Suffixes • Using a Dictionary: Alphabetizing • Recognizing Main Ideas and Details • Recognizing Phrases and Clauses • Recognizing Topics and Main Ideas	• Choosing a Topic • Planning Your Paragraph • Writing the Paragraph • Editing • Rewriting
UNIT 1 BUSINESS		
Chapter 1 **Career Planning** • Introduction: *Cool Jobs* • General Interest: *Finding the Job That's Right for You* • Academic: *Your Major and Career: Myths and Possibilities*	• Guessing the Meanings of New Words: Definitions after *Be* or *Means*; Pictures and Captions • Recognizing Words in Phrases: Phrases with Prepositions • Connecting with the Topic	• Using a Graphic Organizer • Strategy: Determining the Main Idea • Focus: Paragraph Describing Your Ideal Job
Chapter 2 **The Free Enterprise System** • Introduction: *People in Business* • General Interest: *How the Market Works—Supply and Demand* • Academic: *Advertising*	• Guessing the Meanings of New Words: Commas, Dashes, Parentheses; *In Other Words* • Previewing: Having Questions in Mind • Using Topic Sentences	• Strategy: Organizing a Paragraph of Description • Focus: Paragraph Describing an Advertisement

The Mechanics of Writing	Critical Thinking Strategies	Test-Taking Strategies
• Parts of Speech • Parts of Speech: Suffixes	• Guessing the Meanings of New Words • Recognizing Main Ideas and Details • Recognizing Topics and Main Ideas	
UNIT 1 BUSINESS		
• Simple Present • Present Perfect • Time Expressions with the Present Perfect • Simple Past • Gerunds and Infinitives	• Applying Your Knowledge to New Situations • Using a Graphic Organizer	• Locating Key Words
• Prepositions of Place • Present Continuous • Stative Verbs • Using Adjectives • Using Multiple Adjectives	• Making Inferences • Previewing: Having Questions in Mind	• Finding Grammatical Errors

Scope and Sequence

Chapter	Reading Strategies	Writing Strategies
UNIT 2 BIOLOGY		
Chapter 3: Animal Behavior • Introduction: *Animal Tales* • General Interest: *Animal Communication* • Academic: *How do Animals Learn?*	• Guessing the Meanings of New Words: *That Is*; *Such As* and *For Example* • Understanding Punctuation: Quotation Marks and Italics • Previewing for the Topic: Headings • Classifying	• Strategy: Organizing a Paragraph of Process • Focus: Paragraph Describing a Learned Behavior
Chapter 4: Nutrition • Introduction: *McDonald's Around the World* • General Interest: *Eating Bugs is Only Natural* • Academic: *Nutrition Basics*	• Guessing the Meanings of New Words: Using Examples • Understanding Italics • Previewing: Reading the Introduction • Previewing: Figures and Tables	• Strategy: Organizing a Paragraph of Analysis • Focus: Paragraph Analyzing a Diet
UNIT 3 U.S. HISTORY		
Chapter 5: From Settlement to Independence: 1607–1776 • Introduction: *Colonial Americans: Who Were They?* • General Interest: *Famous Colonial Americans* • Academic: *The Road to Rebellion*	• Guessing the Meanings of New Words: Using an Explanation in the Next Sentence • Previewing: Scanning for Years • Previewing: Scanning for Events • Making a Timeline	• Strategy: Writing a Summary • Focus: Paragraph Summarizing a Reading from the Chapter
Chapter 6: A Changing Nation: 1850–1900 • Introduction: *Voices from the Past* • General Interest: *The End of the Frontier* • Academic: *Changing Patterns of Immigration*	• Interpreting Graphs • Finding Specific Support • Using a T-chart • Understanding Cause and Effect	• Strategy: Writing a Paragraph of Comparison • Focus: Paragraph Comparing a Pair of Pictures

The Mechanics of Writing	Critical Thinking Strategies	Test-Taking Strategies
UNIT 2 BIOLOGY		
• Simple Past • Combining Ideas • *When* and *Because* • Adverbials of Time • Using Direct and Indirect Objects • Using Articles: *A, An,* and *The*	• Applying Information • Classifying	• Understanding Pronouns
• Count and Noncount Food Nouns • *Too Much* and *Too Many* • *A Lot Of* and *Not Enough* • Cause and Effect with *If (not) . . . will*	• Forming an Opinion • Previewing: Figures and Tables	• Checking Your Work
UNIT 3 U.S. HISTORY		
• *Can* and *Could* • Causatives: *Force* and *Make* • Summary Writing: Condensing	• Using a Venn Diagram to Show Similarities and Differences	• Paraphrasing
• Transition Words of Contrast • Using *There + Be* • Using Quotations to Support General Statements	• Using a T-chart • Finding Specific Support	• Finding Unstated Details

 Introduction

GETTING STARTED

This chapter is an introduction to college level reading and writing. It is unlike later chapters in that it does not have multiple readings and practice with mechanics. It is designed to provide background and present or review essential reading and writing strategies. In this chapter, students will learn about using a textbook effectively. Students will also practice reading strategies such as figuring out the meanings of new words, keeping a word journal, determining parts of speech, using a dictionary, and recognizing main ideas, topics, details, phrases and clauses. Students will also learn and practice a five-step writing process and produce a paragraph about a favorite book.

READING STRATEGIES

Guessing the Meaning from Context
Keeping a Word Journal
Understanding Parts of Speech
Understanding Parts of Speech: Suffixes
Using a Dictionary: Alphabetizing
Recognizing Main Ideas and Details
Recognizing Phrases and Clauses
Recognizing Topics and Main Ideas

WRITING STRATEGIES

Step A. Choosing a Topic
Step B. Planning Your Paragraph
Step C. Writing the Paragraph
Step D. Editing
Step E. Rewriting

Getting Started Opener, page 1

○ Direct students' attention to the photo.
○ Have students discuss the four questions. This can be done in pairs, in small groups, or as a class.
○ Call on students to share their ideas with the class.

Academic Note:

○ Units and chapters in the Quest series always begin with an opening photo and/or other art. Point out to students that this format accomplishes several purposes: it helps them access background knowledge, helps them anticipate content, and provides an easy way to begin discussing a topic. We can often remember new information better when we connect it to what we already know and anticipate what we might learn.

EXPANSION ACTIVITY: Pair Interview

○ Write three to five questions on the board. Create your own or use the ones below.
  What is your name?
  How many years have you studied English?
  How much time each week do you spend reading for pleasure in your language?
  How much time each week do you spend reading in English?
  What is the hardest thing for you about learning English?
○ Put students in pairs to take turns asking and answering the questions.
○ Call on students to introduce their partners to the class, using their partner's answers to the questions.

🎧 Introduction to Reading

○ Have students read the first three paragraphs on page 2.
○ Ask comprehension questions, such as: *How many readings are there in each chapter of this book? What will the book give suggestions about? What is a good way to read a passage?*
○ Direct students' attention to the photo and ask: *What is she doing? Do you do this to your textbooks?*
○ Have students read the passage silently, or play the audio program and have students follow along silently.

○ Ask comprehension questions, such as: *How do American students use textbooks differently from students in some other countries? Why is it good to mark a textbook? How should you mark a textbook?*
○ Tell students that they will now practice some strategies to help them understand the reading more completely.

READING STRATEGY: Guessing the Meaning from Context

○ Go over the information in the box. You can read it aloud, or have students read it silently.
○ Ask: *Should you use a dictionary to look up all the words you don't understand? What should you do first? How do you know what* pristine *means? Do you have to know the meaning of every word in the reading? Which ones do you need to know?*
○ Direct students' attention to the diagram. Explain that this chart can help students make decisions about using a dictionary.
○ Ask: *If you can guess the meaning of the word, should you look it up? If you can't guess the meaning, what question should you ask yourself?*

A. Guessing the Meaning from Context

○ Go over the directions.
○ Have students write new words in the chart and fill in the bubbles for their answers.
○ Put students in pairs to talk about their charts.
○ Call on students to tell the class about one of the words on their chart and how they answered the questions.

ANSWER KEY

Answers will vary.

B. Guessing the Meaning from Context

○ Go over the directions.
○ Have students write the new words and their guesses about the meanings of the new words.
○ Put students in pairs to share their ideas.
○ Call on students to tell the class a new word they could guess and what they guessed about the meaning of the word.

ANSWER KEY

Answers will vary.

EXPANSION ACTIVITY: Dictionary

○ Elicit examples of words from the reading *Getting the Most Out of a Textbook* that are new to students and write the words on the board.
○ Distribute index cards or strips of paper.
○ Divide the class into groups, assigning each group a different new word from the board.
○ Have students write definitions based on their guesses for the assigned words. Point out that you do not expect their definitions to be perfect because these are new words.
○ Collect the definitions and read them aloud, or have students stand and read their own definitions.
○ Have the class vote on which definition they think is the best for each word.
○ Ask students to look up the words in the dictionary to confirm the definitions they created and voted on.

READING STRATEGY: Keeping a Word Journal

○ Go over the information in the box.
○ Ask: *What do you write in a Word Journal? Why should you keep a Word Journal?*

EXPANSION ACTIVITY: First Journal Entry

○ Have students choose one word that is new to them from the reading and create a word journal entry.
○ Tell students to write this entry in their Word Journals.
○ Put students in pairs to share their entries.

READING STRATEGY: Understanding Parts of Speech

○ Go over the information in the box and the examples.
○ Ask comprehension questions such as: *Which part of speech names a person? Which one is an action word? Which one modifies an adjective or verb? Which one describes a noun? What kind of word often comes before a noun? What kind of word comes after the subject and often has an object?*

C. Understanding Parts of Speech

○ Go over the directions.
○ Have students write the parts of speech on the lines. Remind students to identify the parts of speech without using their dictionaries.
○ Put students in pairs to check their answers.
○ Go over the answers with the class.

ANSWER KEY

1. looks = verb, quite = adverb, colorful = adjective;
2. students = noun, absolutely = adverb, deface = verb, textbooks = noun; 3. essential = adjective, skill = noun, mark = verb

---

READING STRATEGY: Understanding Parts of Speech: Suffixes

○ Go over the information in the box.
○ Ask comprehension questions such as: *What part of speech is indicated by the suffix –able? By the suffix –ly? What is an example of a suffix used for a noun?*

Vocabulary Note:

○ Remind students that they can often guess the meaning of a word if they know the meaning of the base word or another word in the same word family. For example, if students know the word *study*, they can guess that *studious* is similar in meaning.
○ Point out that suffixes often change the part of speech (*study is a verb, student is a noun*), while prefixes often change the meaning (*deface means to ruin the appearance, or "face," of something*).

D. Understanding Parts of Speech: Suffixes

○ Go over the directions.
○ Have students write *n, adj,* or *adv* next to each word and then check their answers with a partner.
○ Go over the answers with the class.

ANSWER KEY

1. n; 2. adv; 3. adj; 4. n; 5. adj; 6. n; 7. adv; 8. adj; 9. n; 10. adv; 11. adj; 12. adj; 13. n; 14. adv; 15. adj; 16. n; 17. n; 18. adj; 19. n; 20. n

ANSWER KEY

1. D; M; D
2. D; D; M
3. D; M; D

READING STRATEGY: Using a Dictionary: Alphabetizing

○ Go over the information in the box.
○ Ask comprehension questions such as: *Which word comes first alphabetically* efficient *or* happiness? *Which word comes second alphabetically* deface *or* difference?

E. Alphabetizing

○ Go over the directions.
○ Have students number the words in each column from 1 to 9 to put the words in alphabetical order.
○ Put students in pairs to check their answers.
○ Go over the answers with the class.

READING STRATEGY: Recognizing Phrases and Clauses

○ Go over the information in the box.
○ Ask: *How is a clause different from a phrase? What are two things a clause must have? Which one can be a complete sentence?*

G. Recognizing Phrases and Clauses

○ Go over the directions.
○ Have students write *P* next to phrases and *C* next to clauses and then compare answers with a partner.
○ Have students change the clauses to sentences.
○ Go over the answers with the class.

ANSWER KEY

Group 1: 1. decide; 2. first; 3. from; 4. full-time;
    5. mark; 6. paragraph; 7. probably;
    8. rainbow; 9. right
Group 2: 1. different; 2. difficult; 3. passage; 4. pen;
    5. reader; 6. review; 7. several; 8. skill;
    9. third
Group 3: 1. efficient; 2. essential; 3. margin; 4. maybe;
    5. messy; 6. much; 7. must; 8. need; 9. never

ANSWER KEY

1. C; 2. P; 3. P; 4. P; 5. C; 6. C; 7. P
Sentences from clauses:
1. They marked the paragraph.
5. It is useful.
6. They don't have time.

READING STRATEGY: Recognizing Main Ideas and Details

○ Go over the information in the box.
○ Ask: *What is the difference between a main idea and a detail? What do details do? Which usually comes first, the main idea or the detail?*

F. Recognizing Main Ideas and Details

○ Go over the directions.
○ Have students write *M* next to the main idea and *D* next to the detail sentences for each group.
○ Put students in pairs to check their answers.
○ Go over the answers with the class.

READING STRATEGY: Recognizing Topics and Main Ideas

○ Go over the information in the box.
○ Ask: *What is a topic? What is a main idea? How is a main idea different from the topic?*

H. Recognizing Topics and Main Ideas

○ Go over the directions.
○ Have students write *T* next to topics and *MI* next to main ideas.
○ Put students in pairs to check their answers.
○ Go over the answers with the class.

ANSWER KEY

1. T; 2. T; 3. T; 4. MI; 5. T; 6. MI; 7. T

Introduction to Writing
○ Go over the information at the top of page 11. Ask: *How many steps does the writing process have? What are they?*

WRITING STRATEGY: Step A. Choosing a Topic
○ Go over the information in the box.
○ Ask: *What are three things your topic should be? Why are these three things important?*

Step A. Choosing a Topic
○ Go over the directions.
○ Have students complete the blanks and answer the questions on page 12.
○ Put students in pairs to practice asking and answering Questions 1 through 5.

ANSWER KEY
Answers will vary.

WRITING STRATEGY: Step B. Planning Your Paragraph
○ Go over the information in the box.
○ Ask: *Where can you get ideas for the paragraph? What else can you do to help your paragraph? What must good paragraphs have?*

Step B. Planning Your Paragraph
○ Have students answer the questions.
○ Put students in pairs to talk about their answers.
○ Call on students to share their ideas with the class.

ANSWER KEY
Answers will vary.

WRITING STRATEGY: Step C. Writing the Paragraph
○ Go over the information in the top half of the box.
○ Ask: *What words help connect one sentence with another? What is an example of a transition word? What are some common problems with first drafts?*
○ Have students read the example of a first draft. Elicit examples of problems with the draft.

Step C. Writing the Paragraph
○ Go over the directions.
○ Have students write paragraphs on their topics. Remind students not to worry about mistakes yet.

WRITING STRATEGY: Step D. Editing
○ Go over the information in the box.
○ Ask: *What is editing? Why should you do it? What are some things to look for when you edit?*

Step D. Editing
○ Go over the directions.
○ Have students use the questions to edit their paragraph from Step C.
○ Have students correct their mistakes.

WRITING STRATEGY: Step E. Rewriting
○ Go over the information in the box. Ask: *What are some questions to ask yourself when you rewrite?*
○ Have students read the example. Elicit examples of mistakes that have been corrected in this revision.

Step E. Rewriting
○ Go over the directions.
○ Have students rewrite their paragraphs.
○ Put students in pairs to read and revise their partner's paragraphs.
○ If necessary, have students rewrite again.
○ Collect the paragraphs.

UNIT 1 ●●●●● BUSINESS

Unit Opener, page 17

○ Direct students' attention to the photo and unit and chapter titles on page 17.
○ Brainstorm ideas for what the unit will include and write students' ideas on the board.

CHAPTER 1 CAREER PLANNING

In this chapter, students will read about different careers, how to prepare for careers, and about college majors. First, students will read about real people who have cool jobs such as an ice cream taster and a toy designer. Then they will learn about how to find the right job by assessing their own strengths, interests, and values. Finally, students will explore the relationship between course work in college, especially in one's major, and future career possibilities. These topics will prepare students to write about their ideal jobs.

VOCABULARY

animator	grow up	major in	television reporter
art gallery director	have a head for	medical illustrator	therapist
be good at	interested in	myth	think about
be interested in	job switching	profile	values
be stuck in	lead to	rehabilitation	
book editor	lifestyle	related to	
facilities	look forward to	self-assessment	

READING STRATEGIES

Connecting with the Topic
Guessing the Meanings of New Words:
    Definitions after *Be* or *Means*
Using a Graphic Organizer
Guessing the Meanings of New Words:
    Pictures and Captions
Recognizing Words in Phrases: Phrases with
    Prepositions

CRITICAL THINKING STRATEGIES

Predicting (Part 1)
Applying Your Knowledge to New Situations (Part 1)
Classifying (Part 2)
Making Connections (Part 3)
Note: Strategy in bold is highlighted in the student book.

MECHANICS

Simple Present
Present Perfect
Time Expressions with Present Perfect
Simple Past
Gerunds and Infinitives

TEST-TAKING STRATEGY

Locating Key Words

WRITING STRATEGY

Determining the Main Idea

CHAPTER 1 Career Planning

Chapter 1 Opener, page 19

○ Direct students' attention to the photo. Ask them what is happening in the photo.
○ Have students discuss the four questions. This can be done in pairs, in small groups, or as a class.
○ Check students' predictions of the chapter topic.

PART 1 INTRODUCTION
COOL JOBS, PAGES 20–24

Before Reading
Thinking Ahead

○ Have students look at the photos and read the questions.
○ Put students in pairs to answer the questions.
○ Call on students to share their ideas with the class.

ANSWER KEY
Answers will vary.

CRITICAL THINKING STRATEGY: Predicting

○ Predicting is an important critical thinking strategy. It allows students to anticipate the content of readings, which in turn promotes comprehension.

EXPANSION ACTIVITY: Category Sort

○ Tell students that you are going to ask some questions. They will respond by moving around the room to stand with classmates who have the same or similar answers. Point out that they should ask classmates questions in order to sort themselves. Encourage students to form distinct groups according to answer.
○ Ask a question: *What is your major?/What do you plan to major in?* Remind students to sort themselves by answer. When students have formed

---

groups, call on someone from each group to tell the class their answer (*Business*).
○ Ask several more questions. Create your own or use the ones below.
What is most important to you in a job?
What type of environment would you like to work in?
What would you like to wear to work?
How long do you want to work in one job?

🎧 Reading

○ Have students look at the reading. Ask: *What is this story about?* (*cool jobs*). Go over the directions and the questions.
○ Have students read the passage silently, or have students follow along silently as you play the audio program.
○ Ask students how the people in the story got their cool jobs and what their qualifications were.

Culture Notes:

○ Ben and Jerry are two real people who started an ice cream company in Vermont. Ben and Jerry and their company have supported a variety of environmental causes including preserving the rain forest.
○ Coney Island is an amusement park in Brooklyn, which is part of New York City. It was one of the largest and most famous amusement parks in the first half of the 20th century.
○ Mattel Toys is an American toy company. The company makes Barbie dolls. Although only about 12 inches tall, Barbie dolls are modeled after adult women. Ruth Handler, a cofounder of Mattel, created the first Barbie doll in 1959 and named the doll after her daughter Barbara.
○ LEGO is a Danish toy company. The company began making toys in 1932, but it wasn't until 1958 that the company began making the type of interlocking building brick toys that LEGO is known for today. The LEGO company sells sets of bricks that can be used to build structures such as houses, stores, cars, and spaceships.

🎧 EXPANSION ACTIVITY: What's Your Reaction?

○ Point out that we often remember more from a reading if we make connections between the ideas in the passage and our own experiences or feelings.
○ Have students read the passage again, or play the audio program again. Have students pause after each profiled person in the reading (or pause the audio program after each profile) and write about their own reactions to each job. Set a time limit of no longer than one minute for each written response.
○ Put students in pairs to talk about their reactions to the different jobs.
○ Call on students to share their ideas with the class.

After Reading

A. Check Your Understanding

○ Go over the directions and the example in the chart.
○ Have students complete the chart with information from the reading.
○ Have students check their answers with a partner.
○ Go over the answers with the class.

ANSWER KEY

Name	Jobs	What They Do	Qualifications
Peter Lind	ice cream taster	develops new ice cream flavors	has culinary experience, likes ice cream, is creative
Anthony Marinaccio	roller coaster operator	greets and seats roller coaster riders	good sense of humor, hard worker, enjoys riding roller coasters, grew up in the area and worked odd jobs in the park when young
Bruce Shelley	computer game designer	designs computer games	designed paper and board games; is curious; likes to solve puzzles; strong in history
Kitty Black Perkins	fashion designer for Barbie dolls	designs doll fashions	is creative; has experience in the design industry
Francie Berger	LEGO designer	creates LEGO structures for stores and toy shows	studied architecture; played with LEGOS since she was three

CRITICAL THINKING STRATEGY: Applying Your Knowledge to New Situations

○ Go over the information in the box.
○ Ask students for examples from the reading of people who used something they already knew in a new situation—their jobs.

B. Using Your Knowledge

○ Go over the directions.
○ Direct students' attention to the words in the box. Make sure students understand each job title.
○ Put students in pairs and have them write the letter of the job title on the correct line for each person in the exercise.
○ Go over the answers with the class.

ANSWER KEY

1. c; 2. e; 3. a; 4. f; 5. d; 6. b

C. Extension

○ Go over the directions.
○ Put students in small groups to make a list of 10 cool jobs and discuss why these are cool.
○ Have students discuss their perfect job and answer the questions in their group.

ANSWER KEY

Answers will vary.

EXPANSION ACTIVITY: Job Ads

❍ Bring in examples of job ads in English. Students can also search online with the phrase "job ads" or go to one of these websites:

http://www.jobads.com/
http://www.careerbuilder.com

You can also have students write their own ads.

❍ Have students use the job ads as models to write an ad for their ideal jobs. Remind students to describe the job and the qualifications.

❍ Put students in pairs to compare job ads.

❍ Call on volunteers to read their ad.

PART GENERAL INTEREST READING

FINDING THE JOB THAT'S RIGHT FOR YOU, PAGES 25–30

Before Reading

READING STRATEGY: Connecting with the Topic

❍ Go over the information in the box.

❍ Direct students' attention to the title of the reading on page 26.

❍ Ask students to think about people they know who love their jobs.

TOEFL® iBT Tip

TOEFL iBT Tip 1: The TOEFL iBT does not directly test the ability to determine the main idea in a text. Instead, examinees are required to recognize the minor, less important ideas that do not belong in a summary; or, they may be required to distinguish between major and minor points of information.

❍ Point out that the strategy for *Connecting with the Topic* can help students distinguish between major and minor points in a text on the TOEFL iBT. Students can apply the strategy to other question types that require reading for basic comprehension: fact and detail, vocabulary, and pronoun reference.

A. Thinking Ahead

❍ Go over the directions.

❍ Put students in pairs to answer the questions.

❍ Call on students to share their ideas with the class.

ANSWER KEY
Answers will vary.

READING STRATEGY: Guessing the Meanings of New Words: Definitions after *Be* or *Means*

❍ Go over the information in the box.

❍ Ask: *What are values? How do you know what the word* values *means?*

B. Guessing the Meanings of New Words

❍ Go over the directions.

❍ Have students underline or highlight any definitions that follow *be* or *means*.

TOEFL® iBT Tip

TOEFL iBT Tip 2: The TOEFL iBT tests the ability to determine the meanings of words in context.

❍ Point out that the reading strategy, *Guessing the Meanings of New Words,* will help students improve their vocabulary for the TOEFL iBT. Remind students that in the reading section of the test, scientific terms and academic vocabulary may be defined in the passage. Definitions of key words and terms will provide useful clues for questions that may be asked on the test, and should be given careful attention.

❍ Useful vocabulary words or terms from this reading include the following: *self-assessment,* and *profile.* Remind students of the strategy in the vocabulary activity that appears on the next page.

On the TOEFL iBT, this question appears in the following format:

The word _____ in the passage is closest in meaning to…

🎧 Reading

❍ Go over the directions and the question.
❍ Have students read the passage silently or follow along silently as you play the audio program.
❍ Ask students what sentences they marked in the reading to answer the question *How do you find a job that you will love?*

ANSWER KEY

Students should highlight the following:
First of all, it helps to know something about people who love their jobs.
Most career counselors agree: to find a job that you will love, you need to do a self-assessment exercise.
The first task is to find out what you do best.
The next step is to think about what you enjoy doing.
Finally, you need to think about your values.
After you've answered all the big questions, the next step is finding jobs that match your profile.

CRITICAL THINKING STRATEGY: Classifying

❍ When we classify, we organize information into groups, classes, or categories. This can help students understand and remember information better.
❍ The following expansion activity, *Ask Yourself* uses this critical thinking strategy.

🌏 EXPANSION ACTIVITY: Ask Yourself

❍ Have students skim the reading to find and write down questions they find.
❍ Explain that there are several types of questions in the reading: questions for researching job satisfaction, questions about interests and skills, and questions about values.
❍ Put students in pairs to classify the questions they copied from the reading.
❍ Have students answer the questions about interests and skills and questions about values. Have students discuss their answers with their partners.

ANSWER KEY

Questions for researching job satisfaction:

How do you find a job like this?
Who are they? (the people who love their jobs)
What are they like?
What's important to them?

Questions about interests and skills:

What am I good at?
What do I like to do?
What classes did you like the most?
In which classes did you get the best grades?
What kinds of tests did you do well on?
What clubs do you belong to?
What sports do you play?
What are your hobbies?

Questions about values:

What are my values?
Do you want to help others?
Do you want to improve the environment?
What are your politics?
Is it important to work with or for people who think as you do?
Is a healthy lifestyle important to you?
Do you want a job that isn't stressful?

After Reading

A. Main Idea

❍ Go over the directions. Have students fill in the bubble next to the main idea. Encourage them to review the reading if necessary.
❍ Go over the answer with the class.

ANSWER KEY

C

 ## B. Vocabulary Check

❍ Go over the directions.
❍ Have students write the meanings of the words on the lines and then check their answers with a partner.
❍ Go over the answers with the class.

ANSWER KEY

1. learning about yourself; 2. things that are important to you in life; 3. the way that you live your life; 4. a list of characteristics that describe you

READING STRATEGY: Using a Graphic Organizer

❍ Go over the information in the box. Ask: *What can graphic organizers help you do?*

TOEFL® iBT Tip

TOEFL iBT Tip 3: The TOEFL iBT tests the ability to understand facts, examples, and explanations in a text; however, it does not directly test understanding of the main idea of a passage.

❍ The *Using a Graphic Organizer* activity in Activity C requires students to visually connect information. This will help to scaffold students' abilities upward toward mastering the schematic table questions on the test.

❍ Remind students that being able to skim and scan to locate information is a technique that will help them with the schematic table question type on the test.

❍ Students will also benefit from doing Activity D, *Critical Thinking*, in order to prepare for the classification or summary question type.

C. Using a Graphic Organizer

❍ Go over the directions.
❍ Have students complete the graphic organizer with a partner.
❍ Go over the answers.

ANSWER KEY
(Answers may vary.)

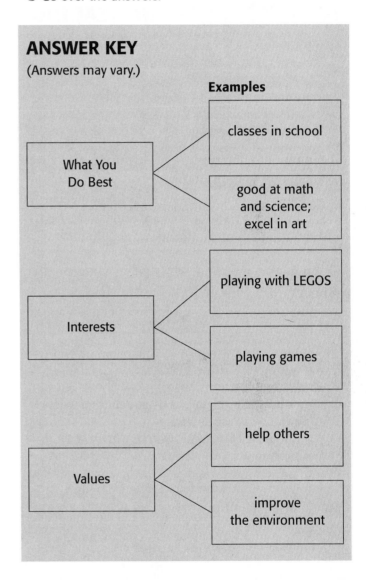

D. Critical Thinking

❍ Go over the directions.
❍ Have students complete the graphic organizer about themselves.
❍ Put students in pairs to compare their answers and discuss possible jobs that would be a good match for each student. Have students write down possible jobs.
❍ Call on students to share their answers with the class.

ANSWER KEY

Answers will vary.

PART ACADEMIC READING
Your Major and Career: Myths and Possibilities, pages 31–37

Before Reading

A. Thinking Ahead

❍ Go over the directions and the questions.
❍ Put students in small groups to discuss the questions.
❍ Call on students to answer the questions.

ANSWER KEY

Answers will vary.

B. Vocabulary Preparation

❍ Go over the directions.
❍ Have students highlight the definitions that follow *be* or *mean* in each sentence.
❍ Have students circle n for *noun* or v for *verb* for the words in red.

ANSWER KEY

Highlight:
1. changing jobs (n)
2. places that provide services (n)
3. treatment to improve a mental or physical problem (n)
4. to be in a situation that you can't get out of (v)
5. to be good at something (v)
6. an incorrect idea (n)
7. to become an adult (v)
8. to expect positive events in the future (v)

Pronunciation Note:

❍ Most suffixes that are used to denote the person who does a particular action do not change the stress pattern of the base word. For example, *report* and *reporter* both have the greatest stress on the second syllable (-*port*).
❍ Adding –*ian*, however, moves the stress to the syllable before the suffix. For example, in *music*, the stress is on the first syllable, but in *musician*, the stress is on the second syllable.

EXPANSION ACTIVITY: Reword It

❍ Explain the activity. You will say a sentence with one of the new vocabulary words or phrases (*Tony did a lot of job switching before he became a writer.*) and call on a student. The student should rephrase the sentence to use the definition in it (*Tony did a lot of changing jobs before he became a writer.*).
❍ Call on a student and say a sentence. Elicit a sentence that uses the definition.
❍ Continue to call on students, or have the student who gave the last definition call on a classmate.
❍ Continue the activity until all the words have been used.

READING STRATEGY: Guessing the Meanings of New Words: Pictures and Captions

❍ Go over the information in the box.
❍ Ask: *Where can we find captions? What is a water quality specialist?*

C. Guessing the Meanings of New Words

❍ Go over the directions.
❍ Have students skim the reading to find new words in captions.
❍ Elicit the words and write them on the board.

TEST-TAKING STRATEGY: Locating Key Words

❍ Go over the information in the box. Ask: *What should you look for in test questions?*

D. Locating Key Words
○ Go over directions.
○ Have students highlight key words in the sentences from Activity A on page 36.

ANSWER KEY
Key words should include: major, career

TOEFL® iBT Tip

TOEFL iBT Tip 4: The TOEFL iBT tests the ability to understand key words contained within a text.

○ Point out that the test-taking strategy, *Locating Key Words,* will help students improve their vocabulary and overall strategies for answering questions on the TOEFL iBT. Locating key words in a sentence and linking them to information in the text will help students build vocabulary and improve their reading skills.

On the TOEFL iBT a vocabulary question may appear in the following format:
   In stating _____ the author means that…

Reading
○ Go over the directions and the question.
○ Have students read the passage silently, or play the audio program and have students follow along silently.
○ Ask how college majors prepare people for careers.

After Reading
A. Check Your Understanding
○ Go over the directions.
○ Have students check the sentences that are true.
○ Go over the answers with the class.

ANSWER KEY
Check: 2, 3, 6

B. Vocabulary Check
○ Go over the directions.
○ Put students in small groups to talk about the jobs listed.
○ Call on students to share their ideas with the class.
○ Have students list three other jobs from the reading. Remind students to look for words with the suffixes *–or*, *–er*, *–ist*, and *–ian*.
○ Elicit the other job titles found in the reading and write them on the board.

ANSWER KEY
Answers may vary. Other jobs in the reading include: Journalist, college career counselor, toy designer, newspaper reporter, speechwriter, general manager of a regional theater, executive director of a chamber music society, music therapist, international business specialist, advertising copywriter, water quality specialist, environmental lawyer, historian, international trade specialist, fashion designer, photographer, certified public accountant, bank manager

EXPANSION ACTIVITY: Career Research
○ Have students choose a career to research. It can be a career mentioned in the reading or just one in which they are interested.
○ Photocopy and distribute the Black Line Master *Career Research* on page BLM 1 for students to use in taking notes on their research topics.
○ Have students conduct research online or at the library to find out what tasks and qualifications are required in that career.
○ Put students in small groups to share their research, or have students present to the class.

C. Finding Important Details
○ Go over the directions.
○ Have students work in pairs to complete the graphic organizer.
○ Go over the answers with the class.

ANSWER KEY

Answers may vary. See below for ideas.
Accounting: bank manager, accountant
Communications: news reporter, advertising copywriter
Environmental science: water quality specialist, environmental lawyer
History and political science: historian, international trade specialist
Visual arts: animator, fashion designer, photographer

READING STRATEGY: Recognizing Words in Phrases: Phrases with Prepositions

○ Go over the information in the box.
○ Ask: *How can you remember the correct preposition?*

 D. Recognizing Words in Phrases: Phrases with Prepositions

○ Go over the directions.
○ Have students fill in the blanks with the correct prepositions.
○ Go over the answers with the class.

ANSWER KEY

1. in; 2. in; 3. at; 4. to; 5. to

CRITICAL THINKING STRATEGY: Making Connections

○ Remind students that making connections is an important critical thinking skill that can help them remember new information.

E. Making Connections

○ Go over the directions.
○ Have students list five career possibilities for the major they choose and then discuss their ideas with a partner.
○ Call on students to share their ideas with the class.

ANSWER KEY

Answers will vary.

F. Word Journal

○ Go over the directions.
○ If needed, review how to keep a Word Journal with the students. Direct students to page 5 in the student book.
○ Have students write important words in their Word Journals.

G. Journal Writing

○ Go over the directions.
○ Explain that this is a quick-writing activity and does not have to be perfect. Point out that journal writing can be a warm-up to a more structured writing assignment, helping to generate ideas.
○ Have students write. Set a time limit of ten minutes.
○ Put students in pairs to read or talk about their writing.

Website Research

○ For additional information on majors and careers, you could direct students to the following websites:
  • Taking the Mystery Out of Majors - Princeton Review
    (http://www.princetonreview.com/college/ research/articles/majors/choosemajor.asp)
  • Ten Facts About Majors and Careers - Stanford University
    (http://cardinalcareers.stanford.edu/majors/ tenfacts.htm)
  • College Majors and Career Information Rutgers University
    (http://careerservices.rutgers.edu/CareerHandouts. html)
  • List of Careers - WisconsinMentor.org
    (http://www.wisconsinmentor.org/career/ CareerCenter/career_clusters.asp)

PART ④ THE MECHANICS OF WRITING, PAGES 38-41

○ Go over the directions.

Simple Present

○ Go over the information in the box about the simple present. Ask: *When do we use the simple present? How do we form the third person singular?*

A. Spelling
○ Review the spelling rules on page 173.
○ Go over the directions.
○ Have students write the third person singular form of each verb.
○ Call on volunteers to write the words on the board or spell them out loud to the class.

ANSWER KEY
1. plays; 2. takes; 3. studies; 4. fixes; 5. plans; 6. wishes; 7. dances; 8. enjoys; 9. does; 10. likes; 11. guesses; 12. goes

B. Simple Present
○ Go over the directions.
○ Have students fill in the blanks with the correct forms of the verbs in parentheses.
○ Go over the answers with the class.

ANSWER KEY
1. lives; 2. goes; 3. studies; 4. enjoys; 5. hopes; 6. works; 7. spends

Present Perfect
○ Go over the information in the box.
○ Ask: *How do we form the present perfect? How is the past participle formed for regular verbs? What is the past participle of go?*

Grammar Notes:
○ The present perfect can be used to talk about things that started in the past and continue in the present, as can the present perfect continuous (*I have been studying English since 1999.*). The present perfect is used with stative, or non-action verbs, such as *be, know, have.* Stative verbs will be discussed in Chapter 2. Most verbs that talk about mental or emotional states or possession are stative verbs. Although some students may be familiar with the present perfect continuous, students will not practice it in this book.

○ We often use the present perfect form of verbs such as *live, work,* and *study* to talk about actions that started in the past and continue in the present.
○ The present perfect is also used with actions that began and ended in the past when the time is not known or not important.

Time Expressions with Present Perfect
○ Go over the information in the box.
○ Ask: *What is an example of a phrase that begins with* since? *A phrase that begins with* for?

C. Present Perfect
○ Go over the directions.
○ Read the first sentence and elicit the correct answer (*has lived*).
○ Have students fill in the blanks with the correct present perfect form of the verbs in parentheses.
○ Go over the answers with the class.

ANSWER KEY
1. has lived; 2. has known; 3. has been; 4. has worked; 5. has gone; 6. have discussed

Simple Past
○ Go over the information in the box.
○ Ask: *When do we use the simple past? How are most regular past tense verbs formed? How do we form the negative in the simple past tense?*

Grammar Notes:
○ You may want to remind students that when we use the simple past, we usually know or state the time.
○ The simple past is used with expressions such as *last night, last week, yesterday, two years ago,* and *after that.*

D. Simple Past
○ Go over the directions.
○ Read the first sentence and elicit the correct form of the verb (*played*).

○ Have students fill in the blanks with the correct forms of the verbs in parentheses.
○ Go over the answers with the class.

ANSWER KEY
1. played; 2. enjoyed; 3. went; 4. took; 5. majored; 6. became

E. Review
○ Go over the directions.
○ Read the first sentence and elicit what tense should be used and why *(is, because they are talking about* now). If helpful, elicit the words in the paragraph that indicate time *(for the past two years, last week, since he was a child)*.
○ Have students complete the paragraph with the correct verb forms. Remind students that they can use any of the three tenses.
○ Go over the answers with the class.

ANSWER KEY
1. is; 2. has gone; 3. saw; 4. discussed; 5. has; 6. has studied; 7. enjoys; 8. has been; 9. took

F. Application
○ Go over the directions.
○ Have students write five sentences about themselves. Remind students to use the questions listed as prompts for their sentences.
○ Put students in pairs to share their sentences.
○ Call on students to read a sentence to the class.

ANSWER KEY
Answers will vary.

Gerunds and Infinitives
○ Go over the information in the box.
○ Ask: *What is an example of a verb that is usually followed by a gerund? Does a gerund or an infinitive usually follow the verb* hope?

G. Gerunds and Infinitives
○ Go over the directions.
○ Read the first sentence and elicit the correct answer (*volunteering*).
○ Have students complete the sentences with a gerund or infinitive.
○ Go over the answers with the class.

ANSWER KEY
1. volunteering; 2. to take; 3. to be; 4. to study; 5. working; 6. spending

TOEFL® iBT Tip

TOEFL iBT Tip 5: Although the TOEFL iBT does not discretely test grammar skills, examinees' essay scores will be determined based on the range of grammar and vocabulary used in their essays.

○ Point out that the grammar activities in *The Mechanics of Writing* part of this chapter will help them improve their use of verb tenses as well as gerunds and infinitives for essay writing.

○ TOEFL iBT essays may be scored higher based on whether or not the examinee can use verb tenses correctly in a sentence. Using verb tenses and more sophisticated phrases will help students improve their overall essay writing.

PART ⑤ ACADEMIC WRITING, PAGES 41–42

Writing Assignment
○ Go over the writing assignment.
○ Have students read the five steps.
○ Direct students' attention to Step A and have students choose a job to write about.
○ Direct students' attention to Step B. Have students answer the questions using short notes.

WRITING STRATEGY: Determining the Main Idea

○ Go over the information in the box.
○ Ask: *How many main ideas are there in one paragraph? What else do you know about paragraphs? What is the main idea in the example?*
○ Ask students to write a sentence that expresses the main idea of the paragraph they are going to write about their ideal job.

○ Direct students' attention to Step C. Have students write paragraphs, using their notes from Step B. Remind students to follow the rules in bullets and to use their main idea sentence.
○ Direct students' attention to Step D. Have students read and edit their paragraphs, looking for mistakes in paragraph form, tenses, gerunds and infinitives, and spelling. Remind students to make sure their main idea is clear, and that all sentences relate to that idea.
○ To encourage peer editing, have students exchange paragraphs with a partner, edit, and return to the writer.
○ Direct students' attention to Step E. Have students rewrite the paragraphs.
○ Collect the paragraphs.

TOEFL® iBT Tip

TOEFL iBT Tip 6: Both the integrated and independent essays of the TOEFL iBT will be scored based on how well the examinee completes the overall writing task. The writing section also requires that the ideas in the essay be connected from paragraph to paragraph.

○ Point out that the *Determining the Main Idea* strategy in *The Academic Writing* part of this chapter will help students improve their writing coherence and ability to link the flow of ideas in their essays. They will need to connect main ideas from paragraph to paragraph in order to demonstrate unity of thought, coherence, and the flow of ideas.

EXPANSION ACTIVITY: Main Ideas in Paragraphs

○ Have students choose one of the readings from this chapter.
○ Ask students to write a sentence expressing the main idea of each paragraph in the reading.

EXPANSION ACTIVITY: Editing Practice

○ Photocopy and distribute the Black Line Master *Editing Practice* on page BLM 2.
○ Go over the directions.
○ Have students correct the mistakes and then compare answers with a partner.
○ Go over the answers with the class.

ANSWER KEY

My ideal career is being a medical illustrator. ~~X~~ T his job is ideal for me because it matches my skills, interests, and values. When I was in college, I major ed in biology and art ∧ I have always love d drawing pictures. I also enjoy ~~to learn~~ learning ∧ about the human body. I even considered ~~to go~~ going ∧ into medicine. When I graduated, I decided ~~going~~ to go ∧ into medical illustration. I ∧ have studied illustration since 2002, so I really understo~~od~~ ∧ and the job now. I have ha~~s~~ d ∧ great practice in my classes, so I expect to get a job soon.

U N I T 1 BUSINESS

CHAPTER 2 THE FREE ENTERPRISE SYSTEM

In this chapter, students will read about an economic system known as the free enterprise system. First, students will read about two successful people who own their own companies: Yvon Chouinard, owner of a company that makes equipment and clothing for outdoor activities, and Oprah Winfrey, who is a talk-show host, TV producer, and publisher. Students will also learn about how the economic market works, and about the laws of supply and demand. Finally students will read about advertising and marketing. These topics will prepare students to write a descriptive paragraph about an ad.

VOCABULARY

advertisement	equilibrium price	mass marketing	retirement
appeal to	the free enterprise system	minority	shortage of
baby boomers	frequent	motivation	spa
consumers	into	multicultural country	surplus
designer labels	the law of demand	multiethnic group	target
determine	the law of supply	multimillion-dollar company	target marketing
dual decision-maker	the market	multinational corporation	trends
enterprise	market segment	multipurpose room	tweens

READING STRATEGIES

Guessing the Meanings of New Words: Using Commas, Dashes, and Parentheses
Previewing: Having Questions in Mind
Guessing the Meanings of New Words: *In Other Words*
Using Topic Sentences

CRITICAL THINKING STRATEGIES

Thinking Ahead (Part 1)
Making Inferences (Part 1)
Making Connections (Part 3)
Note: The strategy in bold is highlighted in the student book.

MECHANICS

Prepositions of Place
Present Continuous
Stative Verbs
Using Adjectives
Using Multiple Adjectives

TEST-TAKING STRATEGY

Finding Grammatical Errors

WRITING STRATEGY

Organizing a Paragraph of Description

CHAPTER 2 The Free Enterprise System

Chapter 2 Opener, page 43

○ Direct students' attention to the photo. Ask them what is happening in the photo.
○ Have students discuss the four questions. This can be done in pairs, in small groups, or as a class.
○ Check students' predictions of the chapter topic.

PART 1 INTRODUCTION
PEOPLE IN BUSINESS, PAGES 44–46

Before Reading

Thinking Ahead

○ Have students look at the photos and read the questions.
○ Put students in pairs to answer the questions.
○ Call on students to share their ideas with the class.

ANSWER KEY

Answers will vary.

CRITICAL THINKING STRATEGY: Thinking Ahead

○ Thinking ahead is an important critical thinking skill. It allows students to anticipate content of readings, which in turn promotes comprehension.

🎧 Reading

○ Have students look at the reading. Go over the directions and the question. Note that students will answer the question in Activity A after the reading.
○ Have students read the passage silently, or have students follow along silently as you play the audio program.

Culture Notes:

○ Yvon Chouinard was born in 1938 in Lewiston, Maine. He invented his first piece of climbing equipment when he was 19. His outdoor-clothing and equipment company, Patagonia, is in Ventura, California.
○ Oprah Winfrey is a famous American television talk-show host. She was born in 1954 in Mississippi. She has been a reporter and an actor. Her company publishes the magazine *O*.

EXPANSION ACTIVITY: Successful Entrepreneurs

○ Put students in pairs to brainstorm characteristics of successful entrepreneurs, or businesspeople.
○ Elicit ideas and write them on the board.
○ Have students use a search engine and enter the words "successful entrepreneurs," or have students do library research on the topic. Ask students to write down characteristics of these successful people in business.
○ Call on students to tell the class what they learned.
○ Note which characteristics students listed were also listed in their research.

After Reading

A. Check Your Understanding

○ Go over the directions.
○ Have students write three answers to the question.
○ Have students discuss their answers with a partner.
○ Go over the answers with the class.

ANSWER KEY

Answers will vary, but might include:
- They both own and operate their own companies.
- They both help others.
- They are wealthy.
- They both enjoy what they do; they don't do it just for money.
- They educate others.

B. Vocabulary Expansion
○ Go over the directions.
○ Put students in pairs to discuss the meanings of the words.
○ Call on students to share their ideas with the class.

Vocabulary Notes:
○ You may want to point out that *multi-* is a prefix, something added to the beginning of a word. Prefixes often alter the meaning, but not the part of speech of a word. For example, *ethnic* is an adjective, as is *multiethnic*.
○ Point out that words beginning with *multi-* are sometimes hyphenated and sometimes not. Both variations can be found in dictionaries.

ANSWER KEY
multimillion-dollar company: a company worth many millions of dollars
multipurpose room: a room used for many different purposes, often for entertainment or exercise
multicultural country: a country with many different cultures
multiethnic group: a group representing many ethnic groups
multinational corporation: a corporation with offices in many countries

CRITICAL-THINKING STRATEGY: Making Inferences
○ Go over the information in the box.
○ Ask: *What does* infer *mean? Do we infer from information that is directly stated?*

C. Making Inferences
○ Go over the directions.
○ In small groups, have students answer the question by making inferences.
○ Call on students to share their ideas with the class.

ANSWER KEY
Answers will vary.

TOEFL® iBT Tip

TOEFL iBT Tip 1: The TOEFL iBT tests the ability to make inferences or draw conclusions based on what is implied in a passage.

○ Point out that the activity *Making Inferences* requires students to draw conclusions and form generalizations based on information presented in the reading.

○ By using key words and phrases from the text, students will be able to make assumptions and apply this skill to the reading section of the TOEFL iBT.

On the TOEFL iBT this question may appear in the format such as:
   Which of the following can be inferred from paragraph __ about _____?

EXPANSION ACTIVITY: Support It
○ Tell students that when we make inferences, we have to base the inferences on some evidence that is stated.
○ Model the activity. Ask a question that involves an inference (*Do you think Oprah is intelligent?*). Elicit support for that inference (*She learned to read when she was very young.*).
○ Put students in pairs to create five questions that involve making inferences from the reading.
○ Put two pairs of students together. Have the pairs take turns asking questions and giving support for answers.
○ Walk around the room to monitor the activity and provide help as needed.

PART ② GENERAL INTEREST READING

HOW THE MARKET WORKS— SUPPLY AND DEMAND, PAGES 47–50

Before Reading

A. Thinking Ahead

- ○ Go over the directions.
- ○ Put students in pairs to answer the questions.
- ○ Call on students to share their ideas with the class.

ANSWER KEY

Answers will vary. Ideas might include:
1. They are customers in a market. The man and woman are buying food from the other man.
2. The seller wants to sell the product and make money. The buyers want to get a good product and save money. They might be negotiating over the price.
3. They will agree on a price, and the couple will buy something.

READING STRATEGY: Guessing the Meanings of New Words: Using Commas, Dashes, and Parentheses

- ○ Go over the information in the box.
- ○ Ask: *What types of punctuation often indicate definitions?*

TOEFL® iBT Tip

TOEFL iBT Tip 2: The TOEFL iBT tests the ability to determine the meaning of words in context.

- ○ Point out that the following activity, *Guessing the Meanings of New Words,* will help students improve their vocabulary for the TOEFL iBT. By identifying words that are used to define or explain other words and understanding their meanings, students will be able to apply this information toward further understanding the concepts presented in the text.

- ○ Remind students that the TOEFL iBT texts will often include glossaries for terms, low-frequency words or specific phrases for which a dictionary might normally be necessary.

On the TOEFL iBT this question appears in the following format:
The word _____ in the passage is closest in meaning to…

B. Guessing the Meanings of New Words

- ○ Go over the directions.
- ○ Have students underline or highlight any definitions that are set off by commas, dashes, or parentheses in the reading.

READING STRATEGY: Previewing: Having Questions in Mind

- ○ Go over the information in the box.
- ○ Point out that each reading in this book has a question to think about. Direct students' attention to the question for the reading passage *How the Market Works—Supply and Demand.*

EXPANSION ACTIVITY: Question It

- ○ Have students preview the reading by looking at the title, the bold-faced words, and by skimming the first and last sentences.
- ○ Have students write three questions they think will be answered in the reading. Ideas might include: *What is the free enterprise system? What are the laws of supply and demand?*
- ○ Put students in pairs to compare questions.
- ○ Call on students to share questions with the class. Write students' questions on the board.

◯ Reading

- ○ Go over the directions and the question. Have students highlight the answer to the question as they read.
- ○ Have students read the passage silently, or have students follow along silently as you play the audio program.

EXPANSION ACTIVITY: Answer It

○ Direct students' attention to the questions on the board from the previous expansion activity *Question It*.
○ Have students answer the questions that were answered in the reading.
○ Go over their answers with the class.

After Reading

A. Main Idea

○ Go over the directions.
○ Ask students what sentences they highlighted in the reading to answer the question *How does the market determine the price of products?*
○ Go over the answers with the class.

ANSWER KEY

Students should highlight the following:
The market determines the price of products by two general rules: the laws of supply and demand.
(lines 11–12)

EXPANSION ACTIVITY: Graphic Organizer

○ Photocopy and distribute the Black Line Master *Graphic Organizer Practice* on page BLM 3.
○ Have students complete the graphic organizer. Remind students that they used a graphic organizer to show important details in Chapter 1.
○ Put students in pairs to compare graphic organizers.
○ Go over the information with the class.

ANSWER KEY

Characteristics of the free enterprise system: individuals can own businesses; the market determines prices
Laws determining price: Law of Supply; Law of Demand
Problems with supply: surplus; shortage

 B. Vocabulary Check

○ Go over the directions.
○ Have students write the meanings on the lines. Remind students not to use a dictionary.
○ Go over the answers with the class.

ANSWER KEY

1. the private enterprise system; 2. a business; 3. the exchange of goods and services by buyers and sellers; 4. people usually buy more of a product when it's at a lower price; 5. producers will usually supply more of a product if they can increase the price; 6. people who buy things; 7. too many; 8. the point where supply and demand meet; 9. not enough

EXPANSION ACTIVITY: Bingo

○ Have students create a 3 by 3 grid on a piece of paper.
○ Ask students to write the following key words and phrases on the grid in any order: *enterprise, the free enterprise system; the market; the law of demand; consumers; the law of supply; surplus; equilibrium price; shortage of.*
○ Remind students how to play bingo: They should try to get three words in a row horizontally, vertically, or diagonally. Students should call out "Bingo" when they have three in a row.
○ Call out the definitions for each word or phrase (from the answer key in Activity B) in random order. Remind students to cross off the words for which they hear definitions.

C. Comprehension Check

○ Direct students' attention to the chart. Ask: *What information is on the chart?*
○ Go over the directions.
○ Have students answer the question.
○ Go over the answer.

ANSWER KEY

95 cents

D. Critical Thinking

○ Point out that applying knowledge is an important critical thinking skill. When we use what we have learned in a reading to understand new information, we apply knowledge.
○ Put students in small groups to discuss the questions.
○ Call on students to share their ideas with the class.

ANSWER KEY

Answers may vary. Ideas may include:
1. The price of coffee or strawberries often goes up when supplies are low, for example, when crops are ruined. The demand would be higher than the supply. The price of computers goes up when the technology is new because there is more demand.
2. The supply of oranges will be limited, so the price will go up. Bald men will want the new cream, so demand will be high, driving the price up.
3. The supply was probably greater than the demand at the original price. By cutting the prices, the store can increase potential demand.

EXPANSION ACTIVITY: Real Reading

○ Bring in headlines or short articles about rising or falling prices, or have students bring articles.
○ Put students in pairs or small groups to talk about what factors might be affecting prices.
○ Call on students to share their ideas with the class.

PART ③ ACADEMIC READING
ADVERTISING,
PAGES 51–57

Before Reading

A. Thinking Ahead

○ Go over the directions. Read the questions aloud.
○ Ask questions about the words in red (*What is an example of a trend? Who is a minority in this country? What is a definition of the phrase appeal to?*).
○ Put students in groups to discuss the questions.
○ Call on students to share ideas.

ANSWER KEY

Answers will vary.

B. Parts of Speech

○ Go over the directions.
○ Read the first sentence. Elicit that *advertise* is a verb. Have students circle the correct part of speech.
○ Have students identify the part of speech of each word in red.
○ Go over the answers with the class.

ANSWER KEY

1. v; 2. n; 3. adj; 4. v; 5. v; 6. n; 7. n; 8. v

EXPANSION ACTIVITY: Use It

○ Have students write original sentences using the words in red from Activity B. Point out that for words that can be more than one part of speech (e.g., *need*), they should try to use the word in two different sentences.
○ Put students in pairs to read their sentences.
○ Call on students to read their sentences to the class.

C. Vocabulary Preparation

○ Go over the directions.
○ Read the first sentence and ask: *What is a baby boomer?* Elicit the answer.
○ Have students highlight the meanings of the words in red.
○ Go over the answers with the class.

ANSWER KEY

Highlight:
1. the 80 million Americans born between 1946 and 1964
2. the time of life when they will stop working, probably after age 65
3. some money and a house after her parents died
4. often visit
5. a wonderful place for a massage or sauna
6. kids ages 8 through 12

READING STRATEGY: Guessing the Meanings of New Words: *In Other Words*
○ Go over the information in the box.

TOEFL® iBT Tip

TOEFL iBT Tip 3: The TOEFL iBT tests the ability to determine the meaning of words in context.

○ Point out that the strategy *Guessing the Meanings of New Words: In Other Words* and Activity D will help students improve their vocabulary for the TOEFL iBT.

○ By identifying words that are used to define or explain other words and understanding their meanings, students will be able to apply this information toward further understanding the concepts presented in the text.

○ Recognizing and being able to use the phrase *in other words* can also be applied to the independent and integrated writing tasks.

D. Guessing the Meanings of New Words
○ Go over the directions.
○ Have students skim the reading to find the phrase *in other words* and highlight the phrase. Have students look for meanings of new words after the phrase.

⌒ Reading
○ Go over the directions and the questions. Point out that students will answer these questions in Activity A after the reading.
○ Have students read the passage silently, or play the audio program and have students follow along silently.
○ Elicit the words that are defined by the phrase *in other words* and what they mean (from Activity D above).

ANSWER KEY
Words defined by the phrase *in other words*:
mass marketing = the advertising of products to a large general market
target = possible buyers for advertisers' products

Culture Notes:
○ Art Weinstein is a professor at Nova Southeastern University in Florida in the Huizenga Business School. His book *Market Segmentation* was published in 2004.
○ McDonald's is a popular fast-food restaurant, known for hamburgers and french fries. Ray Kroc started the first of the McDonald's restaurants in 1955 in Illinois. There are now restaurants in 119 countries.
○ The Census Bureau is an agency of the United States government. It surveys U.S. residents every 10 years, collecting a lot of information about the people in the United States.
○ *Vogue* is a popular fashion magazine.
○ *Entrepreneur* is a magazine for people starting their own businesses.

After Reading
READING STRATEGY: Using Topic Sentences
○ Go over the information in the box.
○ Ask: *What does the topic sentence tell us? Where can you often find the topic sentence?*

TOEFL® iBT Tip

TOEFL iBT Tip 4: The TOEFL iBT does not directly test the ability to determine the main idea in a text. Instead, examinees are required to recognize the minor, less important ideas that do not belong in a summary; or, they may be required to distinguish between major and minor points of information.

○ Point out that the strategy for *Using Topic Sentences* will help students distinguish between major and minor points in a text on the TOEFL iBT and link those ideas throughout the passage.

○ Remind students that this type of question is called a *prose summary* or *classification* question, and partial credit will be given for correct answers. On the TOEFL iBT, the answers to this type of question are not in traditional multiple-choice format.

○ The question type appears in the form of a schematic table that requires examinees to select and drag answer choices to specific positions in a chart.

A. Check Your Understanding

○ Go over the directions.
○ Have students highlight the topic sentences in each paragraph and write answers to the questions.
○ Go over the answers with the class.

ANSWER KEY

1. Advertising is important because different businesses are competing for the same market.
2. Advertisers need to determine a target (possible buyers for their product) and where they should advertise.
3. Advertisers need to think about people's motivations.
4. Target marketing is important.
5. Baby boomers, minorities, tweens

 B. Vocabulary Check

○ Go over the directions and the example.
○ Have students write the correct words or phrases on the lines.
○ Put students in small groups to compare answers.
○ Go over the answers with the class.

ANSWER KEY

1. target; 2. ads; 3. target marketing; 4. market segments; 5. mass marketing; 6. dual decision-maker; 7. motivations

---

EXPANSION ACTIVITY: Flash Cards

○ Tell students that using flash cards can help them remember new vocabulary.
○ Distribute 10 index cards to each student.
○ Model the activity. Write a word or phrase from the chapter on a piece of paper in large letters. Write its definition on the back. Hold up the paper so students can read the word or phrase. Elicit its meaning. Show students the definition on the back of the paper.
○ Have students choose 10 words they want to focus on from the chapter.
○ Tell students to write the word or phrase on one side of the card and its definition on the other.
○ When students have created 10 flash cards, put students in pairs to practice using the flash cards.

 C. Words in Phrases: Phrases with Prepositions

○ Go over the directions and the example.
○ Have students complete the sentences with the missing prepositions.
○ Go over the answers with the class.

ANSWER KEY

1. for; 2. in; 3. on; 4. for; 5. on; 6. for; 7. for; 8. about; 9. on; 10. about

D. Application

○ Go over the directions.
○ Put students in pairs to fill in the chart.
○ Call on students to share their ideas with the class.

ANSWER KEY

Answers may vary.

Ad	What is the product?	Who is the target?	Where might you see the ad?	What might be people's motivation to buy this?
Example: milk ad	milk	middle-aged women	women's magazines	They want to be thinner.
GM ad	car	people who like the outdoors	magazines, especially outdoor magazines	They want adventure.
Kellogg's ad	cereal	parents and kids	in a magazine	Kids might like the tiger. Parents want their kids to have fun.
Tennis ad	tennis products	people who play tennis	sports magazines	They want to be good tennis players.

```
● ● ● ● ● ● ● ● ● ● ● ● ● ● ● ● ● ● ● ●
```
CRITICAL THINKING STRATEGY: Making Connections

○ Remind students that synthesizing, or combining information from different sources, is an important critical thinking skill that can help them remember new information.
```
● ● ● ● ● ● ● ● ● ● ● ● ● ● ● ● ● ● ● ●
```

 E. Making Connections

○ Go over the directions.
○ Have students answer the questions.
○ Call on students to share their ideas with the class.

ANSWER KEY

1. Advertising increases demand.
2. people who like outdoor activities

F. Word Journal

○ Go over the directions.
○ Have students write important words in their Word Journals.

G. Journal Writing

○ Go over the directions.
○ Explain that this is a quick-writing activity and does not have to be perfect. Point out that journal writing can be a warm-up to a more structured writing assignment, helping to generate ideas.
○ Have students write. Set a time limit of 10 minutes.
○ Put students in pairs to read or talk about their writing.

 Website Research

○ For additional information on market segments and target marketing you could direct students to the following websites:
  • Target Marketing—SBA Marketing Basics, U.S. Small Business Administration (http://www.sba.gov/starting_business/marketing/target.html)
  • Finding Customers: Market Segmentation—Ohio State University Fact Sheet (http://ohioline.osu.edu/cd-fact/1253.html)

Academic Notes:

○ Students may have to do research on the Internet for this class or others. You may want to point out that the last three letters on a website address indicate the type of site. For example, .gov stands for government, .org for organization, .edu for an educational institution and .com for a commercial site.
○ In general, governmental and educational sites are more reliable sources of information than commercial sites.

PART ④ THE MECHANICS OF WRITING, PAGES 58–63

○ Go over the directions.

Prepositions of Place

○ Go over the information in the box about prepositions of place. Direct students' attention to the photos and prepositions on page 59.
○ Move around the room and ask questions using prepositions of place (*Who is next to me? Who is in front of you? What is on my desk?*).

A. Prepositions

○ Go over the directions and the example.
○ Have students fill in the blanks with prepositions and prepositional phrases.
○ Go over the answers with the class.

ANSWER KEY

1. on; 2. in front of; 3. in; 4. at the bottom; 5. above; 6. on; 7. in back of; 8. in the background; 9. on; 10. next to; 11. at the bottom of; 12. in the bottom right-hand corner

EXPANSION ACTIVITY: TPR Drawing

❍ Distribute plain paper to students.
❍ Explain the activity. You will give instructions using prepositions of place. Students are to draw what you describe.
❍ Give instructions for drawing a picture (e.g., *First, draw a car in the middle of the paper. Put a tree next to the car. Draw a man between the car and the tree*). Walk around the room to monitor the activity.
❍ Have students compare pictures with a partner.
❍ For more practice, put students in pairs to take turns describing a picture from a book or magazine while their partner draws it.

B. Prepositions

❍ Go over the directions.
❍ Have students write sentences about other ads using prepositions of place.
❍ Call on students to read their sentences to the class.

ANSWER KEY

Answers will vary.

Present Continuous

❍ Go over the information in the box.
❍ Ask: *How many parts are there to the verb in the present continuous? What is the first part? When do we use the present continuous?*

C. Spelling

❍ Go over the directions.
❍ Review the spelling rules for *–ing* words on page 173.
❍ Have students write the *–ing* form of the verb on the lines.
❍ Go over the answers with the class.

ANSWER KEY

1. standing; 2. sitting; 3. kissing; 4. cutting; 5. happening;
6. wearing; 7. hugging; 8. dancing; 9. lying; 10. beginning;
11. dropping; 12. fighting

Stative Verbs

❍ Go over the information in the box.
❍ Ask comprehension questions such as: *What is the stative meaning of* see? *What is the nonstative meaning of* think?

Grammar Notes:

❍ You may want to give students a way to understand and remember stative verbs. Point out that words that describe mental states (*know*) and emotional states (*love*), as well as words that describe perception (*seem*) and ownership (*own*) are usually stative and are not used in the continuous form.
❍ Words that relate to the senses are usually stative if they are describing a quality of something (*That smells good; His skin feels rough.*).

D. Stative Verbs

❍ Go over the directions.
❍ Have students complete the paragraph with the correct form of the verbs in parentheses.
❍ Go over the answers with the class.

ANSWER KEY

1. is standing; 2. think; 3. don't remember; 4. looks;
5. is smiling; 6. wearing/is wearing; 7. has; 8. is resting;
9. seems; 10. guess

E. Stative Verbs

❍ Go over the directions.
❍ Have students write 10 sentences about the ads on pages 51 and 56.
❍ Call on students to read sentences to the class.

ANSWER KEY

Answers will vary.

Using Adjectives/Using Multiple Adjectives

❍ Go over the information in the boxes.
❍ Ask: *Where do we often put adjectives? What do adjectives do? Which word should come first, an adjective of size or color?*

EXPANSION ACTIVITY: Word Sort
○ Distribute index cards or strips of paper to students.
○ Put students in pairs to brainstorm at least three adjectives for each category: opinion, size, condition, age, color, nationality. Walk around the room to monitor the activity and provide help as needed.
○ Have students write each adjective on a strip of paper or index card. Students should make 10 cards or strips.
○ Have each pair exchange their cards or paper strips with another pair of students.
○ Instruct students to create five sentences from the adjectives they received. They should use three adjectives in the correct order in each sentence. Have students write their sentences down on a piece of paper.
○ Call on students to read their sentences to the class.

F. Using Adjectives
○ Go over the directions.
○ Have students write seven sentences about one or more ads using two or more adjectives in each sentence.
○ Call on students to read their sentences to the class.

ANSWER KEY
Answers will vary.

TEST-TAKING STRATEGY: Finding Grammatical Errors
○ Go over the information in the box. Ask: *What is one way to find an error?*

G. Finding the Errors
○ Go over the directions.
○ Have students read the first sentence. Elicit the word or phrase that is incorrect (*D*). Have students circle the letter.
○ Have students circle the letter of the word or phrase that is incorrect in each sentence and then compare answers with a partner.
○ Go over the answers with the class.

ANSWER KEY
1. D; 2. C; 3. A; 4. D

TOEFL® iBT Tip

TOEFL iBT Tip 5: Both the integrated and independent essays of the TOEFL iBT will be scored based on how well the examinee completes the overall writing task. However, the writing section also requires that the essay follow the conventions of spelling, punctuation, and layout.

○ Point out that *Finding the Errors* and other activities in *The Mechanics of Writing* part of this chapter will help students improve their grammar, usage, spelling, and the overall flow of their essays.

PART 5 ACADEMIC WRITING, PAGES 63–64

Writing Assignment
○ Go over the writing assignment.
○ Have students read the five steps.
○ Direct students' attention to Step A and have students choose an ad to write about.
○ Direct students' attention to Step B. Have students answer the questions using short notes.

WRITING STRATEGY: Organizing a Paragraph of Description
○ Go over the information in the box.
○ Ask: *What type of words are especially important in a paragraph of description? What is the topic of the example? What details are included?*

○ Direct students' attention to Step C. Have students write paragraphs, using their notes from Step B. Remind students to follow the rules in the bullets in the Writing Strategy box.

○ Direct students' attention to Step D. Have students read and edit their paragraphs, looking for mistakes in paragraph form, prepositions of place, tenses, stative verbs, spelling, and the order of adjectives. Remind students to check for a main idea, and that all sentences relate to that idea.

○ To encourage peer editing, have students exchange paragraphs with a partner, edit, and return to the writer.

○ Direct students' attention to Step E. Have students rewrite the paragraphs.

○ Collect the paragraphs.

TOEFL® iBT Tip

TOEFL iBT Tip 6: The independent writing task on the TOEFL iBT requires students to think critically about a topic and present their personal preferences or opinions in an organized format.

○ Remind students that the *Writing Strategy: Organizing a Paragraph of Description* is a strategy they will need to use when writing their essays.

○ The independent writing task often requires students to describe an object, idea, or event.

○ The grammar presented in this chapter will be extremely helpful in formalizing a descriptive essay that is coherent and will help students improve their overall writing skills.

EXPANSION ACTIVITY: A Favorite Place

○ Distribute pieces of plain paper.

○ Model the activity. Quickly draw one of your favorite places on the board. Include enough details to describe using prepositions. Tell the class about your place using prepositions and adjectives (*My favorite place when I was a child was my kitchen. The table was next to a big window, and I could look outside at the beautiful tall trees…*).

○ Have students draw a favorite place they have now or a favorite place they had in childhood. Set a five-minute time limit.

○ Put students in pairs to talk about their pictures and their favorite places. Remind students to use prepositions of place to describe this favorite place.

○ For additional writing practice, have students write a paragraph about this place.

EXPANSION ACTIVITY: Editing Practice

○ Photocopy and distribute the Black Line Master *Editing Practice* on page BLM 4.

○ Go over the directions.

○ Have students correct the mistakes and then compare answers with a partner.

○ Go over the answers with the class.

ANSWER KEY

Parents are the target ~~about~~ ^of^ this VISA ad. ~~On~~ ^In^ this ad, three ~~Hispanic young~~ ^young Hispanic^ children are playing in the yard. All three ~~are seeming~~ ^seem^ happy. One girl ~~is having~~ ^has^ a water hose in her hand, and she is spraying water at the other two. She ^is^ spraying an open mailbox. Behind the children is a ~~white large~~ ^large white^ house. The slogan ^"^Kids: Another reason to pay bills automatically with your VISA card" is above ~~to~~ their heads. There's information at the bottom ^of^ the ad.

Unit 1 Vocabulary Workshop

○ Have students review vocabulary from Chapters 1 and 2.

A. Matching

○ Go over the directions.
○ Have students write the correct letters on the lines to match the definitions to the words.
○ Go over the answers.

ANSWER KEY

1. a; 2. e; 3. d; 4. f; 5. c; 6. j; 7. i; 8. h; 9. b; 10. g

B. True or False?

○ Go over the directions.
○ Have students fill in the correct bubble.
○ Go over the answers.

ANSWER KEY

1. F; 2. T; 3. T; 4. F; 5. F; 6. T; 7. F; 8. T

C. Phrases with Prepositions

○ Go over the directions.
○ Have students write the correct prepositions on the lines. Note that students may use some words more than once.
○ Go over the answers.

ANSWER KEY

1. in; 2. at; 3. on; 4. about; 5. for; 6. in; 7. at; 8. about

D. Frequently Used Words

○ Go over the directions.
○ Have students fill in the blanks with words from the box.
○ Go over the answers.

ANSWER KEY

1. child; 2. played; 3. every; 4. worked; 5. Today; 6. get; 7. friendship; 8. years; 9. met; 10. remembered

○ Direct students' attention to the photo and unit and chapter titles on page 67.
○ Brainstorm ideas for what the unit will include and write students' ideas on the board.

CHAPTER 3 ANIMAL BEHAVIOR

In this chapter, students will study animal behavior, specifically learned behavior. First, students will read about learned behavior in an octopus and a young tiger. Then, students will read about how animals such as monkeys, apes, and dolphins communicate. Finally, students will learn about the differences between innate, or genetically determined behavior, and learned behavior such as habituation, imprinting, trial and error, association, and insight. These topics will prepare students to write about a learned behavior and the process by which it was learned.

VOCABULARY

adaptable	cub	imprinting	observation	territoriality
apes	distinct	innate	piglet	trial-and-error
association	dolphins	insight	prey on	the wild
behavior	fetch	instinct	reflex	
calls	fight-or-flight response	jackdaw	salivate	
captivity	gestures	language	suckle	
conditioning	habituation	migration	syntax	

READING STRATEGIES

Understanding Punctuation: Quotation Marks and Italics
Previewing for the Topic: Headings
Guessing the Meanings of New Words: *That Is*
Classifying
Guessing the Meanings of New Words:
　　Such As and *For Example*

CRITICAL THINKING STRATEGIES

Thinking Ahead (Part 1)
Applying Information (Part 3)
Making Connections (Part 3)
Note: The strategy in bold is highlighted in the student
　　book.

MECHANICS

Simple Past
Combining Ideas
Using Direct and Indirect Objects
Using Articles: *A, An,* and *The*

TEST-TAKING STRATEGY

Understanding Pronouns

WRITING STRATEGY

Organizing a Paragraph of Process

CHAPTER 3 Animal Behavior

Chapter 3 Opener, page 69

❍ Direct students' attention to the photo. Ask them what is happening in the photo.
❍ Have students discuss the four questions. This can be done in pairs, in small groups, or as a class.
❍ Check students' predictions of the chapter topic.

PART ❶ INTRODUCTION
ANIMAL TALES,
PAGES 70–72

Before Reading

Thinking Ahead

❍ Have students look at the photos and read the questions.
❍ Put students in pairs to answer the questions.
❍ Call on students to share their ideas with the class.

CRITICAL THINKING STRATEGY:
Thinking Ahead

❍ Tell students that thinking ahead is an important critical thinking strategy. It allows students to anticipate the content of readings, which in turn promotes comprehension.

ANSWER KEY

Answers may vary. See ideas below.
1. (first and second questions) monkeys, cows, lions, geese; (third question) monkeys live in Africa, Asia, and South America, cattle live everywhere, lions are in Africa, geese live everywhere, but the man looks like he is in Asia;
2. grooming; walking in a line; hunting; being guided by a man;
3. Answers will vary.

EXPANSION ACTIVITY: Animal Folktales

❍ Point out that many cultures have folktales about animals, and often the tale demonstrates the animal's intelligence or some other characteristic (e.g., *In African folktales, Anansi the spider demonstrates cleverness*).
❍ Put students in pairs to brainstorm animal tales they know and to write them down in a list.
❍ Have each pair select from their list one animal tale that illustrates a particular quality of that animal.
❍ Have the pairs take notes to help them retell the story.
❍ Have each pair retell their story to another pair of students.
❍ In a variation, put students in pairs or small groups to act out an animal tale for the class. The number in the group will depend on the number of characters in the story.

🎧 Reading

❍ Have students look at the reading. Go over the directions and the questions.
❍ Have students read the passage silently, or have students follow along silently as you play the audio program.

Culture Note:

❍ *Best Friends Magazine* has articles about animals, wildlife, and the natural world.

EXPANSION ACTIVITY: Make a Personal Connection

❍ Remind students that we often remember more from a reading if we make connections between the ideas in the passage and our own experiences or feelings.

○ Have students choose the animal story in the reading that they liked best. Ask students to write for one minute on the reasons why they liked the animal story they chose. If necessary, ask questions to help prompt students: *Which animal did you think was smarter? Which one do you find more interesting? Which animal would you like to spend time with?*

○ Put students in pairs to share their ideas.

○ Call on students to share their ideas with the class.

After Reading

A. Check Your Understanding

○ Go over the directions.

○ Have students answer the questions in small groups.

○ Go over the answers with the class.

ANSWER KEY

1. The octopus learned to open jars of its favorite food.

2. The tiger doesn't eat the pigs because he grew up with them.

 ### B. Vocabulary Expansion

○ Go over the directions.

○ Have students answer the questions.

○ Go over the answers with the class.

ANSWER KEY

1. piglet; 2. cub

READING STRATEGY: Understanding Punctuation: Quotation Marks and Italics

○ Go over the information in the box.

○ Ask: *Why do we use quotation marks? What are three reasons for using italics?*

TOEFL® iBT Tip

TOEFL iBT Tip 1: The TOEFL iBT requires examinees to paraphrase and cite information from written and spoken sources on the integrated writing skills essay. Understanding punctuation in a reading text can serve as an example that students can learn to replicate in their own work.

○ Point out that the punctuation activities following the *Understanding Punctuation* strategy will help students understand vocabulary, quoted information, and titles that the author uses in a passage.

○ Remind students that they will also be able to apply these strategies to writing their essays, particularly when they are required to paraphrase or quote parts of a text.

C. Understanding: Punctuation

○ Go over the directions.

○ Direct students' attention to the use of quotation marks and italics in the reading.

○ Have students answer the questions with a partner.

○ Go over the answers with the class.

ANSWER KEY

1. to quote someone's exact words; 2. The italics are used for a magazine title (*Best Friends Magazine*) and for emphasis (*their, his, too*). The quotation marks are used for a word that really means something different (*brother*).

PART ② GENERAL INTEREST READING
ANIMAL COMMUNICATION, PAGES 73–77

Before Reading
A. Thinking Ahead
○ Go over the directions.
○ Put students in small groups to answer the questions.
○ Call on students to share their ideas with the class.

ANSWER KEY
1. dog and ants; 2. The dog is going to fetch the ball when the person throws it.; The ants are carrying leaves.; 3. Answers will vary.; 4. Answers will vary.

B. Vocabulary Preparation
○ Go over the directions.
○ Have students underline or highlight the meanings of the words in red.
○ Go over the answers with the class.

ANSWER KEY
Highlight:
1. sounds
2. specific and different from the others
3. gorillas and chimpanzees
4. movements with their hands
5. go and get

READING STRATEGY: Previewing for the Topic: Headings
○ Go over the information in the box.
○ Have students preview the reading. Ask: *What do the headings tell you about the reading? What are some new or important words?*

C. Previewing for the Topic
○ Go over the directions.
○ Have students write the five headings in the reading.
○ Go over the answers with the class.

ANSWER KEY
Ways that Animals Communicate; Humans; Monkeys and Apes in the Wild; Apes in Captivity; Dolphins in Captivity

READING STRATEGY: Guessing the Meanings of New Words: *That Is*
○ Go over the information in the box.
○ Ask: *What does the phrase* that is *mean? When do we use it? In the example, what does* American Sign Language *mean?*

TOEFL® iBT Tip

TOEFL iBT Tip 2: TOEFL iBT tests the ability to determine the meaning of words in context.

○ Point out that Activity D, *Guessing the Meanings of New Words,* will help students improve their vocabulary for the TOEFL iBT. By identifying words that are given as examples and understanding their meanings, students will be able to apply this information toward further understanding the concepts presented in the text.

○ Mention that the phrase *that is* could become a distracter for students who do not recognize this phrase as a signal for the definition of a word.

EXPANSION ACTIVITY: Sentence Writing

○ Have students use the sentences from Activity B and rewrite each to use *that is* (e.g., *One kind of African monkey has three calls—that is, sounds—to other monkeys in the group.*). Note that students can use *that is* with dashes, commas and parentheses.

○ Give students five to ten minutes to rewrite the sentences.

○ Have students share sentences with a partner.

○ Go over the sentences with the class.

○ For greater challenge, have students write original sentences using the vocabulary words from Activity B and the phrase *that is* (e.g., *Birds also use calls—that is, sounds—to communicate with each other.*).

ANSWER KEY

1. One kind of African monkey has three calls—that is, sounds—to other monkeys in the group.
2. Each call is distinct—that is, specific and different from others.
3. In Africa, apes—that is, gorillas and chimpanzees—communicate in many of the same ways that humans do.
4. They use body movements, gestures—that is, movements with their hands—and calls.
5. They learned verbs such as *throw, touch,* and *fetch*—that is, go and get.

D. Guessing the Meanings of New Words

○ Go over the directions.

○ Have students skim the reading to find and highlight the phrase *that is* each time it occurs in the reading.

○ Elicit the words that are defined by the phrase *that is (language, wild, prey on, captivity, syntax).*

Culture Note:

○ American Sign Language is one form of sign language, a system of gestures and grammar that allows hearing-impaired people and others to communicate. Sign language is not universal—there are different forms in different parts of the world.

 Reading

○ Go over the directions and the questions.

○ Have students read the passage silently or follow along silently as you play the audio program.

EXPANSION ACTIVITY: Internet Research

○ Have students go to one of the websites listed on page 40 of the Teacher's Edition. Have students write down three things they learn about animal communication.

○ Call on students to share their ideas with the class.

After Reading

A. Check Your Understanding

○ Go over the directions.

○ Have students answer the questions and then compare answers with a partner.

○ Go over the answers with the class.

ANSWER KEY

1. Animals communicate through smell, special movements, sound, body movements, gestures, calls, and language.
2. Chimps and gorillas can make words in sign language.
3. Dolphins can understand syntax, or grammar rules of word order.

 B. Vocabulary Check

○ Go over the directions.

○ Have students write the words or phrases on the lines.

○ Go over the answers with the class.

ANSWER KEY

1. language; 2. the wild; 3. prey on; 4. captivity; 5. syntax

EXPANSION ACTIVITY: Picture It

○ Model the activity. Draw a picture of one of the words from this chapter (use words from the list on page 31 of the Teacher's Edition). Tell students the part of speech of the word (e.g., *noun*). Students should try to guess as you draw, and keep guessing until someone has guessed the correct word.

○ Explain to students that it is now their turn to draw and that you will assign a word to be drawn. You may want to list these words on the board in particular: *apes, behavior, calls, captivity, cub, distinct, fetch, gestures, innate, jackdaw, language, migration, observation, piglet, prey on, suckle, the wild.*

○ Divide the class into two teams.

○ Call a member from each team to the board. Whisper one of the words from the chapter to each student. Tell the class the part of speech of the word they are going to try to guess.

○ Have the two students draw the word on the board. Their teammates should try to guess the word being drawn. The first team to correctly name the word earns a point.

○ Continue the activity with different students drawing other words from the chapter.

○ In a variation, have students act out the word instead of drawing it.

READING STRATEGY: Classifying

○ Go over the information in the box. Ask: *What do you do when you classify?*

○ Point out that classifying is also a critical thinking strategy, because it requires the reader to notice how things are alike.

TOEFL® iBT Tip

TOEFL iBT Tip 3: The TOEFL iBT tests the ability to recognize organization and purpose in a passage. Examinees are required to recognize the minor, less important ideas that do not belong in a summary; or, they may be required to distinguish between major and minor points of information and apply them to a table or chart.

○ Point out that the strategy for *Classifying* will help students distinguish between major and minor points in a text on the TOEFL iBT.

○ Explain to students that this type of question is called a *prose summary* or *classification* question, and partial credit will be given for correct answers. On the TOEFL iBT, the answers to this type of question are not in traditional multiple-choice format.

○ The question type appears in the form of a schematic table that requires examinees to select and drag answer choices to specific positions in a chart.

C. Classifying

○ Go over the directions.
○ Put students in small groups to complete the chart.
○ Go over the answers.

ANSWER KEY

Fish	Insects	Mammals		Birds
salmon	ant	cat	human	chicken
shark	bee	chimp	monkey	duck
tuna	cockroach	dog	pig	eagle
	termite	dolphin	tiger	goose
		elephant	whale	pigeon
		gorilla		vulture

EXPANSION ACTIVITY: Venn Diagrams

❍ Photocopy and distribute the Black Line Master *Compare and Contrast* on page BLM 5 of the Teacher's Edition.

❍ Have students choose two classes of animals from Activity C (e.g., *fish* and *insects*).

❍ Have students complete the Venn diagram to compare and contrast the two groups. Remind students that the overlapping middle section is for characteristics the two animal classes have in common, and that the areas on the left and right are for the characteristics of the one on that side only.

❍ Put students in pairs to share ideas.

❍ Call on students to tell one quality the two animal classes share and one quality that is unique to one animal class.

PART ③ ACADEMIC READING
HOW DO ANIMALS LEARN?, PAGES 78–85

Before Reading

A. Previewing

❍ Go over the directions. Remind students of the Reading Strategy they learned (on page 74 in the student book) of noticing headings and words in bold.

❍ Have students write the six headings.

❍ Elicit the headings from the class.

ANSWER KEY

Innate Behavior, Habituation, Imprinting, Trial and Error, Association, Insight

B. Vocabulary Preparation

❍ Go over the directions.

❍ Read the first sentence. Elicit the part of speech of *behavior* (n). Have students circle the correct parts of speech.

❍ Go over the answers with the class.

ANSWER KEY

1. n; 2. n; 3. n; 4. v; 5. adj

EXPANSION ACTIVITY: Word Families

❍ Explain that students can increase their vocabulary by learning word families—words that are formed from the same base word.

❍ Say a familiar word that has different variations (*teach*). Elicit other words with the same base word (*teacher, teachable, teachings*).

❍ Point out that we can often find words in a word family that are different parts of speech (*teacher is a noun, while teachable is an adjective*).

❍ Have students create word families for the words in Activity B. Encourage students to use a dictionary if they have difficulty. Tell students that one of the words from Activity B will not form other words.

❍ Put students in pairs to compare ideas.

❍ Call on students to share their ideas with the class.

ANSWER KEY

behavior: behave (v); behavioral (adj)
jackdaw: (none)
association: associate (v), associate (n), associative (adj)
salivate: saliva (n), salivary (adj), salivation (n)
adaptable: adapt (v), adaptation (n), adaptive (adj)

READING STRATEGY: Guessing the Meanings of New Words: *Such As* and *For Example*

❍ Go over the information in the box.

❍ Ask: *What can help you figure out a new word or idea? What phrases do we use to introduce examples?*

C. Guessing the Meanings of New Words

❍ Go over the directions.

❍ Have students underline or highlight the phrases *such as* and *for example* in the reading.

EXPANSION ACTIVITY: Applying Reading Strategies

○ Elicit the reading strategies students have used so far to figure out new words (*using commas, dashes, parentheses, the phrase* that is, *the verb* be).

○ Have students skim the reading *How Do Animals Learn?* to find examples of words they can figure out using these strategies and to write down the words, their meanings, and the strategies used to determine the word meaning.

○ Elicit the words, meanings, and strategies and write them on the board.

ANSWER KEY

behavior—the way animals act (the verb *be*)
innate—born with (*that is*)
blink—quickly close and open eyes (dash, *that is*)
territory—a place that they "own" (dash)
migration—movement of animals from one part of the world to another (commas, the verb *be*)
jackdaw—a kind of bird (dash)
association—putting together different ideas (dash, *that is*)
salivate—produce liquid in the mouth (parentheses)
observation—watching another animal (dash, *that is*)
adaptable—able to change in a new situation (dash, *that is*)

∩ Reading

○ Go over the directions and the question.

○ Have students read the passage silently, or play the audio program and have students follow along silently.

Culture Notes:

○ Ivan Pavlov was born in Russia in 1849. He studied physiology and specifically how digestion worked. This led him to the conditioned reflex studies for which he is famous.

○ Pavlov was a scientist who received a Nobel prize in science. Nobel prizes are prizes awarded to people who have made great achievements in their fields.

After Reading

A. Vocabulary Check

○ Go over the directions.

○ Have students write the letter of the correct answer on the line.

○ Go over the answers with the class.

ANSWER KEY

1. e; 2. d; 3. c; 4. b; 5. a; 6. f

B. Vocabulary Expansion

○ Go over the directions.

○ Have students write the words on the lines.

○ Go over the answers with the class.

ANSWER KEY

a. blink; b. seasonally; c. nest; d. liquid; e. humans; f. adaptable

C. Main Idea and Details

○ Go over the directions.

○ Have students complete the graphic organizer.

○ Go over the answers with the class.

ANSWER KEY

Animal Behavior Includes

Learned behavior such as
1. habituation
2. imprinting
3. trial and error
4. association—examples: conditioning, observation
5. insight

innate behavior such as
1. simple—examples: reflex, fight-or-flight response
2. instinct—examples: territoriality; migration

TEST-TAKING STRATEGY: Understanding Pronouns

○ Go over the information in the box.
○ Ask: *What are some examples of pronouns? What does a pronoun do? What steps should you follow to find the correct pronoun?*

TOEFL® iBT Tip

TOEFL iBT Tip 4: The TOEFL iBT measures the ability to identify the relationships between pronouns and their antecedents (words that come before) or postcedents (words that follow) in a passage.

○ Point out that the Test-taking strategy and activity for *Understanding Pronouns* will help students improve their ability to correctly identify and link pronouns and nouns on the TOEFL iBT.

On the TOEFL iBT this question may appear in the following format:
The word _____ in the passage refers to…

EXPANSION ACTIVITY: Listening for Pronouns

○ Have students write the pronouns *he, she, they,* and *it* on separate pieces of paper.
○ Explain the activity. You will read sentences that are missing pronouns. You will say "blank" when there should be a pronoun. When you pause at the end of the sentence, students should hold up the appropriate pronoun.
○ Read the sentences that follow. Say "blank" where there are blank lines and continue the sentence.
○ Ask students to hold up the pronoun they think should replace the blank. Wait for students to hold up the appropriate pronoun.
○ Encourage students to look around and self-correct.
○ Read the sentence again with the correct pronoun and continue.
The weather keeps changing every day. _____ is hard to predict. (it)
Her grandfather is having a birthday party.

_____ *will be 100 years old! (he)*
My parents are coming to visit next week.
_____ *live in Tampa. (they)*
My favorite movie is The Matrix. _____ *is really exciting. (it)*
His wife was very late. _____ *had a car accident. (she)*
I want to meet Lisa and Frank Martin.
_____ *moved into the house next door. (they)*
Mary has a new car. _____ *is red. (it)*

D. Pronouns

○ Go over the directions.
○ Have students fill in the bubble for the noun or noun phrase the pronoun refers to in each question.
○ Go over the answers with the class.

ANSWER KEY

1. A; 2. C; 3. A; 4. A

CRITICAL THINKING STRATEGY: Applying Information

○ Go over the information in the box. Point out that Activity E will give students practice with this skill.

E. Application

○ Go over the directions.
○ Have students write the type of learned behavior on the lines.
○ Go over the answers with the class.

Culture Note:

○ Konrad Lorenz was born in 1903 in Vienna, Austria. He studied innate behavior in birds. He also wrote a book *On Aggression,* in which he argued that aggressiveness is innate, or instinctual, in humans.

ANSWER KEY

1. imprinting; 2. habituation; 3. association; 4. insight

CRITICAL THINKING STRATEGY: Making Connections

○ Remind students that synthesizing, or combining information from different sources, is an important critical thinking strategy that can help them remember new information.

F. Making Connections

○ Go over the directions.
○ Have students answer the questions and then compare answers with a partner.
○ Call on students to share their ideas with the class.

ANSWER KEY

1. The octopus learned to open the jar through association, specifically through observation of the zoo keepers. The tiger learning to not eat pigs through imprinting.
2. Humans can learn to use language through trial and error, association, and insight. There is also an innate component to language learning.

G. Expansion

○ Go over the directions.
○ Have students think for a few minutes about an example of a learned behavior experienced in their own lives.
○ Have students move around the classroom and ask three classmates the interview question. Students should write notes on the answers their classmates give them.
○ Call on volunteers to share examples of learned behavior they heard about in their interviews.

ANSWER KEY

Answers will vary.

H. Word Journal

○ Go over the directions.
○ Have students write important words in their Word Journals.

I. Journal Writing

○ Go over the directions.
○ Explain that this is a quick-writing activity and does not have to be perfect. Point out that journal writing can be a warm-up to a more structured writing assignment, helping to generate ideas.
○ Have students write. Set a time limit of 10 minutes.
○ Put students in pairs to read or talk about their writing.

Website Research

○ For additional information on animal folktales, you could direct students to:
  • Animal Myths—Oban's Myths and Legends, Planet OzKids
    (http://www.planetozkids.com/oban/legends.htm/)
○ For additional information on animal behavior, learning and communication:
  • The Animal Communication Project—Stephen Hert
    (http://acp.eugraph.com)
  • Animal Learning, Language and Communication—King's Psychology Network
    (http://psyking.net/id31.htm)
  • Animal Learning—Encyclopedia Britannica online
    (http://www.britannica.com/eb/article-9106476)
  • Animal Behavior-Instincts—Encyclopedia of Psychology
    (http://www.psycology.org/links/Environment_Behavior_Relationships/Animal_Behavior_Instincts/)

PART ④ THE MECHANICS OF WRITING, PAGES 86–89

○ Go over the directions.

Simple Past

○ Go over the information in the box about the simple past. Ask: *When do we use the simple past? How do we form the past tense of regular verbs? How do we form the negative in the simple past?*

A. Simple Past
○ Go over the directions. Read the first sentence and elicit the correct form of the verb (*was*).
○ Have students write the past tense form of the verbs in parentheses.
○ Call on volunteers to write the words on the board or spell them out loud to the class.

ANSWER KEY
1. was; 2. had; 3. was; 4. found; 5. brought; 6. named; 7. made; 8. seemed; 9. didn't like; 10. hid; 11. attacked; 12. got; 13. became

Combining Ideas
○ Go over the information in the box.
○ Ask: *What can you join with the word* and? *What do you join with* when *or* because? *What are some words or phrases we can use to put actions in time order?*

EXPANSION ACTIVITY: Everyday Activities
○ Brainstorm a list of everyday activities or processes and write students' ideas on the board (e.g., *getting ready for work, making coffee, taking the bus, doing laundry, preparing a meal, going grocery shopping*).
○ Put students in pairs or small groups to describe the activity in a paragraph using words to combine ideas. Have a student in each pair or group write down the paragraph.
○ Call on representatives from each group to read the paragraph to the class. Have students jot down the words from the box they hear.

B. Combining Ideas
○ Go over the directions and the example.
○ Have students combine the other sentences using words from the box that combine ideas.
○ Go over the answers with the class.

ANSWER KEY
1. She tells jokes and she sometimes tells lies.
2. The dolphins learned nouns, verbs, and prepositions.
3. The chimp was able to reach the bananas when he found a way to use boxes as a ladder.
4. The dolphin carefully watched the arm signals. Then she swam over to the ball.
5. The octopus watched the humans. After a while, she figured out how to open the jars herself.
6. The chimp signed to herself, her doll, and other animals.

Using Direct and Indirect Objects
○ Go over the information in the box.
○ Ask comprehension questions such as: *Where do we put direct objects? What is an indirect object? In the sentence "I gave Lee the book" which noun is the direct object and which the indirect object?*

Grammar Notes:
○ Direct objects receive the action of the verb. In other words, the action is performed on the object.
○ Transitive verbs must have an object; otherwise the thought is incomplete. Intransitive verbs do not need an object, although some intransitive verbs can sometimes take one (*We ate./We ate dinner.*).
○ Some verbs must have a direct object and an indirect object (e.g., *put*).

C. Direct and Indirect Objects
○ Go over the directions and the example.
○ Have students rewrite the sentences, changing the order of the two objects and adding or removing *to.*
○ Go over the answers with the class.

ANSWER KEY
1. Brad gave the dog some food.
2. Bring the ball to me.
3. Patterson has taught Koko ASL.
4. Betty's strategy was to teach the dolphins arm signals.
5. Lance gave some food to the cat.
6. Jen taught American Sign Language to a young chimp.

Using Articles: *A, An,* and *The*

❍ Go over the information in the box.
❍ Ask comprehension questions such as: *Where do we put articles? When we talk about a noun for the first time, what article do we use?*

Academic Note:

❍ You may want to point out that academic texts often discuss ideas and abstractions that don't require an article (*Democracy is an important principle in American society.*). Similarly, when we make generalizations in academic texts, we often use plural nouns without articles (*Apes communicate in many of the same ways as humans.*).

Grammar Notes:

❍ You may want to remind students that we use *an* before nouns beginning with a vowel.
❍ You may want to review some facts about count and noncount nouns. Count nouns can be singular or plural. When singular, they must be preceded by an article, possessive or demonstrative. When plural, they do not need articles, although they may be preceded by one.
❍ Noncount nouns do not require articles, although they may have articles. They are always singular. Noncount nouns are often things that are too large or too small to be counted (*air, sand*) or may be ideas (*honesty, intelligence*).

D. Using Articles

❍ Go over the directions.
❍ Direct students' attention to the first line, and elicit the article that should go before *ocean* (*the*) and the reason *why* (*There is only one ocean by California.*).
❍ Have students fill in the blanks with the correct articles.
❍ Have students check their answers with a partner.
❍ Go over the answers with the class.

ANSWER KEY

1. the; 2. the; 3. a; 4. the; 5. The; 6. a; 7. a; 8. the; 9. the; 10. the; 11. a; 12. the; 13. a; 14. the

E. Review/Editing

❍ Go over the directions.
❍ Have students find and correct the mistakes and then compare ideas with a partner.
❍ Go over the answers with the class.

ANSWER KEY

Forty-five years ago, ~~the~~ *a* young anthropologist went to Gombe, in Tanzania, to study chimpanzees in the wild. Her name was Jane Goodall. At first, she didn't ~~got~~ *get* close to the chimps, because they were afraid of her. Later on they ~~begin~~ *began* to feel comfortable around her and she was able to learn surprising things about them. For example, she learned that wild chimps create tools/ *and* make war.

TOEFL® iBT Tip

TOEFL iBT Tip 5: Both the integrated and independent essays of the TOEFL iBT will be scored based on how well the examinee completes the overall writing task. However, the writing section also requires that the essay follow the conventions of spelling, punctuation, and layout.

❍ Point out that the *Review/Editing* activity in *The Mechanics of Writing* part of this chapter will help students improve their grammar, usage, spelling, and the overall flow of their essays.

PART 5 ACADEMIC WRITING, PAGES 90–91

Writing Assignment
- ○ Go over the writing assignment.
- ○ Have students read the five steps.
- ○ Direct students' attention to Step A and have students choose a behavior to write about.
- ○ Direct students' attention to Step B. Have students answer the questions using short notes.

WRITING STRATEGY: Organizing a Paragraph of Process
- ○ Go over the information in the box.
- ○ Ask: *What is a paragraph of process? How is it organized? What are some transition words you might use?*
- ○ Go over the example. Ask: *What is the main idea of the paragraph? What transition words did the writer use?*

- ○ Direct students' attention to Step C. Have students write paragraphs, using their notes from Step B.
- ○ Direct students' attention to Step D. Have students read and edit their paragraphs, looking for mistakes in paragraph form, the topic sentence, the order of steps, the simple past tense, the use of articles, and transition words and punctuation for them.
- ○ To encourage peer editing, have students exchange paragraphs with a partner, edit, and return to the writer.
- ○ Direct students' attention to Step E. Have students rewrite the paragraphs.
- ○ Collect the paragraphs.

TOEFL® iBT Tip

TOEFL iBT Tip 6: Both the integrated and independent essays of the TOEFL iBT will be scored based on how well the examinee completes the overall writing task.

- ○ Point out that the writing strategy *Organizing a Paragraph of Process* in this chapter will help students improve their writing coherence and ability to link the flow of ideas in their essays by taking smaller steps in their essay development. The "process writing" approach will help students organize their thoughts and take meaningful steps toward developing their essays.

- ○ Remind students that working slowly with sentence-by-sentence combinations will help them develop their paragraphs more concisely, improve the organization of the essay, and likely improve their overall essay scores.

EXPANSION ACTIVITY: Order It
- ○ Have students rewrite their paragraphs from Part 5 on strips of paper, writing one sentence on each strip. Tell students to leave out all words that combine ideas. (student book page 87)
- ○ Put students in pairs to exchange strips.
- ○ Have students recreate their partner's paragraph, insert missing words, and then check the order with the partner.

UNIT 2

●●●●● BIOLOGY

CHAPTER 4 NUTRITION

In this chapter, students will learn about nutrition. In the first reading, students will learn about how the fast-food restaurant chain McDonald's offers different food in different countries to respond to a culture's preferences. Next, students will read about the history and practice of eating insects. In the last reading, students will learn basic facts about nutrition, focusing on six different nutrients. These readings will prepare the students to write a paragraph of analysis about a diet.

VOCABULARY

aquatic	fat	pesticides	tissue
aristocrats	feed	porridge	tradition
ascorbic acid	IU	protein	vitamins
carbohydrates	mg	retinol	
culinary	minerals	survive	
entomology	nutrients	taboo	

READING STRATEGIES

Understanding Italics
Previewing: Reading the Introduction
Previewing Figures and Tables
Guessing the Meanings of New Words: Using Examples

CRITICAL THINKING STRATEGY

Thinking Ahead (Part 1)
Forming an Opinion (Part 1)
Making Connections (Part 2)
Note: Strategy in bold is highlighted in the student book.

MECHANICS

Count and Noncount Food Nouns
Too Much and *Too Many*
A Lot Of and *Not Enough*
Cause and Effect with *If (not) … will*

TEST-TAKING STRATEGY

Checking Your Work

WRITING STRATEGY

Organizing a Paragraph of Analysis

C H A P T E R 4 Nutrition

Chapter 4 Opener, page 93

❍ Direct students' attention to the photo. Ask them what they see in the photo.
❍ Have students discuss the four questions. This can be done in pairs, in small groups, or as a class.
❍ Check students' predictions of the chapter topic.

PART ① INTRODUCTION McDonald's Around the World, pages 94–97

Before Reading

CRITICAL THINKING STRATEGY: Thinking Ahead
❍ Thinking Ahead is an important critical thinking strategy. It allows students to anticipate content of readings, which in turn promotes comprehension.

Thinking Ahead

❍ Have students look at the photos and read the questions.
❍ Put students in pairs to answer the questions.
❍ Call on students to share their ideas with the class.

ANSWER KEY

Answers will vary.

Reading

❍ Have students look at the reading. Go over the directions and the question. Note that students will answer the question in Activity A after the reading.
❍ Have students read the passage silently, or have students follow along silently as you play the audio program.

EXPANSION ACTIVITY: Compare and Contrast
❍ Put students in pairs to brainstorm a list of menu items served at a McDonald's near you. Then have students brainstorm menu items for another restaurant chain (in your local area if possible).
❍ Have students work individually to create Venn diagrams comparing and contrasting the two restaurant chains, and then have them compare diagrams with their partners.
❍ Call on students to tell the class something similar and different about the two restaurants.

After Reading

A. Main Idea
❍ Go over the directions.
❍ Have students discuss and answer the question with a partner.
❍ Go over the answer with the class.

ANSWER KEY

Answers will vary, but should be similar to: McDonald's tries to adapt to the food preferences of different cultures by offering different foods to match each culture's tastes and customs.

B. Finding Details
❍ Go over the directions.
❍ Have students match the food preferences to the countries and then compare answers with a partner.
❍ Go over the answers with the class.

ANSWER KEY

1. a; 2. b; 3. d; 4. c

TOEFL® iBT Tip

TOEFL iBT Tip 1: The TOEFL iBT does not directly test the ability to determine the main idea in a text. Instead, examinees are required to recognize the minor, less important ideas that do not belong in a summary; or, they may be required to distinguish between major and minor points of information.

○ Point out that Activity A, *Main Idea* and Activity B, *Finding Details* will help students distinguish between major and minor points in a text on the TOEFL iBT.

○ Explain to students that this type of question is called a *prose summary* or *classification* question, and partial credit will be given for correct answers. On the TOEFL iBT, the answers to this type of question are not in traditional multiple-choice format.

READING STRATEGY: Understanding Italics

○ Go over the information in the box. Ask: *What are two reasons writers use italics?*
○ Remind students that italics are also used for titles.

C. Understanding Italics

○ Go over the directions.
○ Have students answer the questions.
○ Go over the answers with the class.

ANSWER KEY

1. ayran; 2. local

CRITICAL-THINKING STRATEGY: Forming an Opinion

○ Go over the information in the box.
○ Ask: *What is an opinion? What should you have to support opinions? Why?*

TOEFL® iBT Tip

TOEFL iBT Tip 2: The TOEFL iBT tests the ability to read a passage, listen to a lecture related to that passage, and then write in response to a question based on the two stimuli. This integrated writing skill requires students to think critically about material that they have read, interpret that information and relate it to a lecture, then present ideas in essay format.

○ Remind students that by making comparisons between things and forming an opinion the information can be further applied in the next parts of this chapter: *The Mechanics of Writing* and *Academic Writing.*

○ The independent writing question will often require the examinee to articulate and justify an opinion about an important issue or a preference, and support that opinion with specific references based on personal knowledge and experience.

D. Forming an Opinion

○ Go over the directions.
○ Put students in pairs to discuss the questions.
○ Call on students to share their ideas with the class.

ANSWER KEY

Answers will vary.

EXPANSION ACTIVITY: Agree or Disagree?

○ Write *Agree* on one side of the board and *Disagree* on the other.
○ Call a group of students to the board. Tell students that you will read some statements of opinion, and the students at the board should move to the *Agree* side if they agree and the *Disagree* side if they disagree.
○ Read a statement of opinion (e.g., *There are too many fast-food restaurants.*). Remind students at the board to move, then ask students to explain why they agree or disagree.

○ Read a couple more opinions and have students move.

○ Continue the activity with other groups of students.

○ You can create your own statements or use the ones below.

People should eat at home, not at restaurants.

It is the responsibility of the restaurant to serve healthy food.

Governments should regulate what is on the menu at restaurants.

American fast-food restaurants are destroying the food culture in other countries.

At some point in the future, food will be the same around the world.

Some cultures have healthier diets than others.

PART GENERAL INTEREST READING
EATING BUGS IS ONLY NATURAL, PAGES 97–100

Before Reading

A. Thinking Ahead

○ Go over the directions.

○ Put students in small groups to answer the questions.

○ Call on students to share their ideas with the class.

ANSWER KEY

Answers will vary.

B. Vocabulary Preparation

○ Go over the directions. Elicit what should be highlighted in the first sentence (*the study of insects*).

○ Have students highlight the meanings of the words in red and then compare answers with a partner.

○ Go over the answers with the class.

ANSWER KEY

Highlight:
1. the study of insects
2. wealthy people
3. a grain dish
4. not allowed
5. live in water
6. animal food
7. poisons that kill insects
8. to stay alive
9. custom
10. good to cook and eat

READING STRATEGY: Previewing: Reading the Introduction

○ Go over the information in the box.

○ Ask: *Where do we usually find the introduction? What does it often state?*

TOEFL® iBT Tip

TOEFL iBT Tip 3: The TOEFL iBT does not directly test the ability to determine the main idea in a text. Instead, examinees are required to recognize the minor, less important ideas that do not belong in a summary; or, they may be required to distinguish between major and minor points of information.

○ Point out that the strategy *Previewing: Reading the Introduction* will help students get the overall gist of a text.

○ This strategy can also help for higher level question types, such as insert text questions because students will be able to better identify organization of the text.

C. Reading the Introduction

❍ Go over the directions.
❍ Have students discuss and answer the questions with a partner.
❍ Go over the answers with the class.

ANSWER KEY

1. eating bugs; 2. history of eating bugs and the cultures that still eat bugs today

D. Using Pictures and Captions

❍ Go over the directions. Have students look at the pictures and captions
❍ Call on students to tell the class which of the bugs names are new to them.

🎧 EXPANSION ACTIVITY: Bingo

❍ Have students create a 3 by 3 grid on a sheet of paper.
❍ Ask students to write nine of the definitions in Activity B in random order on the grid, one definition per square.
❍ Remind students of how to play bingo: they should try to get three in a row horizontally, vertically, or diagonally. Students should call out "Bingo" when they have marked three in a row.
❍ Tell students that you will play the audio program or read the passage. When students hear the word that matches a definition on the grid, they should mark the square.

🎧 Reading

❍ Go over the directions and the questions.
❍ Have students read the passage silently, or have students follow along silently as you play the audio program.
❍ Ask students what sentences they highlighted in the reading to answer the questions: *Who eats bugs? Are bugs a healthy food?*

Culture Notes:

❍ John the Baptist is a figure in the New Testament, the part of the Bible that Christians believe in. He is Jesus' cousin, and he baptized people with water as a way to prepare them for Jesus' coming.
❍ The Paiutes are a Native-American tribe that lived in the western part of the United States.
❍ Ghana is a country in Africa.
❍ New Guinea is in the Pacific Ocean, near Australia and Indonesia.
❍ Aboriginal Australians is a term that refers to the people who lived in Australia before it was colonized by the British. It is similar to the expression "Native American."

After Reading

A. Check Your Understanding

❍ Go over the directions.
❍ Have students write their answers to the questions and then compare answers with a partner.
❍ Go over the answers with the class.

ANSWER KEY

1. Romans and Greeks ate bugs in the past, as did Jews and Christians. People eat bugs today in Africa, Asia, and North America.
2. Three reasons that people should eat bugs are that bugs are higher in protein and lower in fat than some other protein sources, they are more economical, and by eating bugs we can help the environment by eliminating pesticides.

EXPANSION ACTIVITY: Graphic Organizer

❍ Photocopy and distribute the Black Line Master *Finding Examples* on page BLM 6.
❍ Have students complete the graphic organizer. Remind students that they used a graphic organizer to show important details in Chapter 1.
❍ Put students in pairs to compare graphic organizers.
❍ Go over the information with the class.

ANSWER KEY

Africa: termites/winged termites; Asia and Australia: aquatic insects, bee larvae, dragonflies, grubs; North/Latin America: agave worm, cicadas, tarantulas, ants

B. Making Inferences

○ Go over the directions.
○ Have students discuss the questions in small groups.
○ Go over the answers with the class.

ANSWER KEY

- Protein is something that is in meat and insects. Yes, protein is a good thing that people should eat. It makes bugs a healthy food.
- Fatty acids are also in food. Some fatty acids are good for you. Unsaturated fatty acids are better for you than other kinds.
- insects

C. Vocabulary Expansion

○ Go over the directions.
○ Have students find the word that means *eaten* and an expression that means *ate*.
○ Go over the answers.

ANSWER KEY

1. enjoyed; 2. dined on

CRITICAL THINKING STRATEGY: Making Connections

○ Point out that making connections between ideas is an important critical thinking strategy that can help students remember new information.

D. Making Connections

○ Put students in pairs to create McDonald's dishes with insects for the cultures listed.
○ Call on students to share their ideas with the class.

ANSWER KEY

Answers may vary.

EXPANSION ACTIVITY: Recipe Research

○ Have students research recipes for a culture other than their own, which uses a food they think is strange or unusual. Students can go online and enter the name of a culture and "recipes." They can also go to the library to look at cookbooks, or ask someone from another culture for a recipe. Alternatively, you could bring in recipes from other cultures to distribute to students.
○ Ask students to bring in one recipe for a food they find unusual from another culture.
○ Put students in small groups to share their recipes.
○ Call on representatives from each group to tell the class about what recipes they found unusual and why.

PART ③ ACADEMIC READING
NUTRITION BASICS,
PAGES 101–108

Before Reading

A. Thinking Ahead

○ Go over the directions.
○ Have students complete the chart.
○ Put students in pairs to talk about their charts and check if their foods are healthy or not.
○ Call on students to tell the class about something their partner eats that is healthy, and why.

ANSWER KEY

Answers will vary.

READING STRATEGY: Previewing: Figures and Tables

○ Go over the information in the box.
○ Ask: *What are figures? What are tables? How can these visuals help you?*

B. Using Figures and Tables

❍ Go over the directions.
❍ Have students answer the questions.
❍ Go over the answers with the class.

ANSWER KEY

1. B; 2. C; 3. B; 4. C

EXPANSION ACTIVITY: Details in Figures and Tables

❍ Have students work in pairs to write five questions based on factual details in the figures and tables in the reading. They should write at least one question about each figure and table.
❍ Have two pairs of students exchange questions. Each pair should answer the questions the other pair wrote.
❍ Have students check their answers with the pair that wrote the questions.

READING STRATEGY: Guessing the Meanings of New Words: Using Examples

❍ Go over the information in the box. Ask: *Where can we find examples?*

TOEFL® iBT Tip

TOEFL iBT Tip 4: TOEFL iBT tests the ability to determine the meaning of words in context.

❍ Point out that the activity *Guessing the Meanings of New Words* will help students improve their vocabulary for the TOEFL iBT. Identifying the meanings of words placed in *apposition to* (next to) other words, or words used as examples with phrases like *such as, for example, for instance, that is* will help students build vocabulary.

❍ Useful vocabulary words or terms from the reading include the following: *nutrients, sugars,* and *fats*.

On the TOEFL iBT this question appears in the following format:

The word _____ *in the passage is closest in meaning to…*

C. Guessing the Meanings of New Words

❍ Go over the directions.
❍ Have students skim the reading to find the phrases *and other* and *for instance*. Students can highlight or write down the examples to help them remember where they are in the reading.
❍ Go over the examples that help explain other words.

ANSWER KEY

Example	word explained by example
bone, muscle, and skin	tissues
chicken	meats
bread and fruit	foods that contain starches and sugars
ascorbic acid, retinol	chemical names

🎧 Reading

❍ Go over the directions and the questions.
❍ Have students read the passage silently, or play the audio program and have students follow along silently.
❍ Ask students what they highlighted to answer the reading questions.

Pronunciation Note:

❍ You may want to point out the intonation pattern we use in saying the items in a list. We use rising intonation on every item followed by a comma, and falling intonation on the last item. For example, when we say *There is a lot of fat in whole milk, butter and cheese,* our voices go up on *milk* and *butter*, and down on *cheese*.

After Reading

A. Main Idea

❍ Go over the directions.
❍ Have students discuss and write down answers with a partner.
❍ Go over the answers with the class.

ANSWER KEY

The six nutrients are: proteins, fats, carbohydrates, vitamins, minerals, and water

B. Finding Details

❍ Go over the directions.
❍ Have students complete the graphic organizer. Note that more than one answer may be correct.
❍ Go over the answers with the class.

ANSWER KEY

Answers may vary. Examples include the following:
Nutrients:

Why the Body Needs Them	Examples
Proteins: to build and repair body parts	meats, fish / eggs, nuts
Fats: to supply body with energy	butter / oils, salad dressing
Carbohydrates: to supply the body with energy	bread / fruit
Vitamins: to help body tissue grow and repair	A, B1, B2, B3 / C, D
Minerals: help blood, bones, teeth, muscle contractions, nerves, thyroid gland	iron, calcium, magnesium / iodine, sodium

C. Vocabulary Check

❍ Go over the directions and the example.
❍ Have students match the nutrition terms in the box with their meanings.
❍ Go over the answers with the class.

ANSWER KEY

Meanings	Nutrition Terms
chemicals your body needs, such as vitamins	nutrients
nutrients that build and repair body parts	proteins
bone, muscle, and skin	tissue
nutrients that supply your body with energy (two words)	fats/carbohydrates
chemicals that help body tissue grow and repair	vitamins
another name for vitamin C	ascorbic acid
another name for vitamin A	retinol
an abbreviation for international units	IU
an abbreviation for milligrams	mg

D. Using Your Knowledge

❍ Go over the directions.
❍ Have students look at their charts on page 101 and make changes if necessary.
❍ Call on students to share what they changed with the class.

ANSWER KEY

Answers will vary.

E. Word Journal

❍ Go over the directions.
❍ Have students write important words in their Word Journals.

F. Journal Writing

○ Go over the directions.

○ Explain that this is a quick-writing activity and does not have to be perfect. Point out that journal writing can be a warm-up to a more structured writing assignment, helping to generate ideas.

○ Have students write. Set a time limit of 10 minutes.

○ Put students in pairs to read or talk about their writing.

 Website Research

○ For additional information on nutrition:
  • USDA Dietary Guidelines
    (http://www.health.gov/dietaryguidelines/)
  • Nutrition Guidelines Summary – CDC, Healthy Youth!
    (http://www.cdc.gov/HealthyYouth/nutrition/guidelines/summary.htm)
  • Nutrition Guidelines Safer Child, Inc.
    (http://www.saferchild.org/nutritio.htm)

 **PART 4 THE MECHANICS OF WRITING, PAGES 109–112**

○ Go over the directions.

Count and Noncount Food Nouns

○ Go over the information in the box about count and noncount food nouns. Ask comprehension questions such as: *What forms can a count noun have? What about noncount nouns? Which can we use* a *or* an *with? When can* coffee *be a count noun? When can* vitamin *be a count noun?*

....

Grammar Notes:

○ You may want to review other information about count and noncount food nouns. Point out that liquids, powders, and grains are usually noncount.

○ Remind students that some food nouns are count nouns when we are talking about the whole thing (*two pizzas, three hams*), but noncount nouns when we are talking about what we might eat (*pizza is delicious, ham is fattening*).

....

A. Count and Noncount Food Nouns

○ Go over the directions and the example.

○ Have students circle the correct answers.

○ Go over the answers with the class.

ANSWER KEY

1. count; 2. noncount; 3. count; 4. count; 5. noncount; 6. noncount

B. Talking About Food

○ Go over the directions and the example.

○ Put students in pairs to practice conversations about what they ate yesterday.

○ Call on students to tell the class about what their partner ate yesterday.

ANSWER KEY

Answers will vary.

EXPANSION ACTIVITY: Alphabet Brainstorm

○ Explain the activity: Students will work in small groups to work their way through the alphabet, listing as many food words as they can for each letter.

○ Give an example. Say the letter *A*, and elicit food nouns (e.g., *apples, avocadoes*). Write the words on the board and elicit which are count nouns and which noncount. Write a *C* next to the count nouns and an *N* next to the noncount nouns.

○ Put students in small groups to list food words for each letter of the alphabet and identify each word they list as count or noncount.

○ Set a time limit of 10 minutes.

○ Call on students to share their ideas with the class.

○ If you want to make this activity competitive, award points to groups that list more words for each letter than the other groups.

Too Much and *Too Many*
○ Go over the information in the box.
○ Ask: *Do we use* too much *or* too many *with count nouns? If I am talking about tea, which expression should I use? If I am talking about apples, which should I use?*

C. *Too Much* and *Too Many*
○ Go over the directions.
○ Have students write the correct phrase on the lines
○ Go over the answers with the class.

ANSWER KEY
1. too many; 2. too much; 3. too much; 4. too many; 5. too many

A Lot Of and *Not Enough*
○ Go over the information in the box.
○ Ask: *Which expression do you use if you have an amount that's too little? Which expression is similar to* many?

Grammar Notes:
○ You may want to reinforce the distinctions between *much, many,* and *a lot of.*
○ *A lot of* can be used in affirmative and negative statements, as well as in questions with both count and noncount nouns.
○ *Many* is used with count nouns in affirmative and negative statements and in questions.
○ *Much* can be used in expressions with *too,* and in questions and negative statements. It is not used in affirmative statements unless it is used with *too.*

D. *A Lot Of* and *Not Enough*
○ Go over the directions and the example.
○ Have students write sentences using the cues.
○ Go over the answers with the class.

ANSWER KEY
1. Alex eats a lot of fruit.
2. James doesn't drink enough milk.
3. You don't take enough vitamin A.
4. Bill eats a lot of chili peppers.
5. Rafael doesn't eat enough fish.
6. Rick and Sara don't take enough vitamins.

Cause and Effect with *If (not)…will*
○ Go over the information in the box.
○ Ask: *When do we often use expressions with if (not)…will? When you are not sure about an effect, should you use* will *or* can?
○ Remind students to use a comma if the *if* clause is first in the sentence.

E. Cause and Effect with *If (not)…Will*
○ Go over the directions and the example.
○ Have students write sentences on the lines about the cause and effect relationships.
○ Call on students to read sentences to the class.

ANSWER KEY
If you eat too many cookies, you will get sick.
If you don't take enough vitamins, you will feel tired.
If you eat a lot of vegetables, you will feel good.
If you drink too much coffee, you will become nervous.
If you drink a lot of milk, you'll have strong bones.

TOEFL® iBT Tip

TOEFL iBT Tip 5: Although the TOEFL iBT does not discretely test grammar skills, examinees' essay scores will be determined based on the range of grammar and vocabulary used in their essays.

○ Point out that the grammar activities in *The Mechanics of Writing* part of this chapter will help them improve their abilities to write descriptive or cause/effect type essays by using nouns and expressions of quantity, as well as conditional forms.

EXPANSION ACTIVITY: Question and Answer

○ Give students five minutes to review the reading *Nutrition Basics* (pages 103–106).

○ Model the activity. Ask a question using the form *What will happen if…* (e.g., *What will happen if you don't drink enough milk?*). Elicit one or more answers (e.g, *If you don't drink enough milk, you won't have strong bones*).

○ Have students write five questions using the reading in the same way.

○ Put students in pairs to practice asking and answering the questions. Walk around the room to monitor the activity and provide help as needed.

○ Call on students to ask a classmate a question.

F. Review: Editing

○ Go over the directions.

○ Have students find and correct the mistakes and then compare answers with a partner.

○ Go over the answers with the class.

ANSWER KEY

Can you eat ~~a~~ nutritious food at a fast-food restaurant? The experts disagree, but some say that if you eat too ~~many~~ *much* fast food, you *will* not have a well-balanced diet. Other nutritionists say that if you make ~~a~~ good choices, you can eat well at a fast-food restaurant. These experts have the following recommendations: Don't add extra sauces, too ~~many~~ *much* cheese, or bacon~~s~~ to your burger. Try your burger with lettuce~~s~~, onion, and tomato, instead. And most importantly, order small or medium sizes—not "super sizes."

PART 5 ACADEMIC WRITING, PAGES 113–114

Writing Assignment

○ Go over the writing assignment.

○ Have students read the five steps.

○ Direct students' attention to Step A, and have students choose a diet to write about.

○ Direct students' attention to Step B. Have students answer the questions using short notes.

WRITING STRATEGY: Organizing a Paragraph of Analysis

○ Go over the information in the box.

○ Ask: *What can you do in the first step? What should you do next? What do you do in the analysis part of the paragraph?*

○ Direct students' attention to the example. Give students time to read the example paragraph. Ask: *What is the writer's opinion about Tony's diet? What are some reasons the writer gives? How does the writer explain the reasons he lists?*

TOEFL® iBT Tip

TOEFL iBT Tip 6: Both the integrated and independent essays of the TOEFL iBT will be scored based on how well the examinee completes the overall writing task.

○ Point out that the *Organizing a Paragraph of Analysis* strategy will help students improve their coherence and the flow of ideas in their independent essays by taking smaller steps in their essay development.

○ Remind students that working at the paragraph level and demonstrating the ability to support their opinions more concisely will likely improve their overall essay scores.

Independent writing tasks may require that examinees analyze an idea, present an opinion or perception about a topic, or develop an argument about a controversial issue. Essay statements may be phrased in a form such as the following:

Do you agree or disagree with the following statement? OR *Some people believe {X} while other people believe {Y}. Which of these positions do you agree with?*

○ Direct students' attention to Step C. Have students write paragraphs, using their notes from Step B. Remind students to follow the steps in the writing strategy.

TEST-TAKING STRATEGY: Checking Your Work
○ Go over the information in the box.
○ Point out that students will do this kind of checking when they edit their paragraphs in Step D.
○ Point out that students should always leave time to check their work on a test, even if they are not writing paragraphs.

○ Direct students' attention to Step D. Have students read and edit their paragraphs, looking for mistakes in paragraph form, the topic sentence, the use of reasons, count and noncount nouns, quantity expressions, and cause/effect statements.
○ To encourage peer editing, have students exchange paragraphs with a partner, edit, and return to the writer.
○ Direct students' attention to Step E. Have students rewrite the paragraphs.
○ Collect the paragraphs.

EXPANSION ACTIVITY: Editing Practice
○ Photocopy and distribute the Black Line Master *Editing Practice* on page BLM 7.
○ Go over the directions.
○ Have students correct the mistakes and then compare answers with a partner.
○ Go over the answers with the class.

ANSWER KEY
Linda has a healthy diet, but she could improve it. Her diet is healthy because she eats a lot of fruits and vegetables. Fruits and vegetables have vitamins. If you get a lot of vitamins, you ~~won't~~ will be healthy. Linda doesn't eat too ~~many~~ much butter or other fatty foods. If you eat too ~~many~~ much fat, you will gain weight. Linda is a vegetarian, so she doesn't eat any meat. Meat is a good source of protein. If you don't get ~~too much~~ enough protein, you might have health problems. Linda needs to eat more protein. She can eat nuts or beans to get more protein.

Unit 2 Vocabulary Workshop

○ Have students review vocabulary from Chapters 3 and 4.

A. Matching

○ Go over the directions.
○ Have students write the correct letters on the lines to match the definitions to the words.
○ Go over the answers.

ANSWER KEY

1. b; 2. e; 3. c; 4. g; 5. i; 6. a; 7. h; 8. d; 9. j; 10. f

B. True or False?

○ Go over the directions.
○ Have students fill in the correct bubble.
○ Go over the answers.

ANSWER KEY

1. T; 2. F; 3. T; 4. T; 5. T; 6. T; 7. F; 8. F

C. Words in Phrases

○ Go over the directions.
○ Have students write the words from the box on the lines to complete the phrases.
○ Go over the answers.

ANSWER KEY

1. movements
2. response
3. error
4. acids
5. products

D. Frequently Used Words

○ Go over the directions.
○ Have students fill in the blanks with words from the box. Note that students may use some words twice.
○ Have students check their answers in the second paragraph on page 71.
○ Go over the answers.

ANSWER KEY

1. arms; 2. pull; 3. rocks; 4. floor; 5. strong; 6. opinion; 7. Glass; 8. exist; 9. natural; 10. watched; 11. human; 12. glass; 13. watching; 14. off

UNIT 3

●●●●● U.S. HISTORY

○ Direct students' attention to the photo and unit and chapter titles on page 117.
○ Brainstorm ideas for what the unit will include and write students' ideas on the board.

CHAPTER 5 FROM SETTLEMENT TO INDEPENDENCE: 1607–1776

In this chapter, students will learn about the early history of the United States. In the first passage, students will read about the early settlers who came from Europe, England, and Africa to settle in the colonies. Next, students will learn about two famous Colonial Americans: Benjamin Franklin, a man who would have a big role in the new country, and Phillis Wheatley, an African slave who became a poet. In the last passage, students will learn of the events that led up to the American Revolution. These readings will prepare students to write a summary paragraph about academic material from the chapter.

VOCABULARY

autobiography	exception	Patriot	quit	theory
boycott	grievances	printer	repealed	trade
colonies	lightning rod	printing shop	retire	unite
curious	Loyalist	protest	smuggle	writs of assistance

READING STRATEGIES

Guessing the Meanings of New Words: Using an Explanation in the Next Sentence
Previewing: Scanning for Years
Previewing: Scanning for Events
Making a Timeline

CRITICAL THINKING STRATEGIES

Thinking Ahead (Part 1)
Using a Venn Diagram to Show Similarities and Differences (Part 2)
Making Connections (Part 3)
Note: The strategy in bold is highlighted in the student book.

MECHANICS

Can and *Could*
Causatives: *Force* and *Make*
Summary Writing: Condensing

TEST-TAKING STRATEGY

Paraphrasing

WRITING STRATEGY

Writing a Summary

CHAPTER 5 From Settlement to Independence: 1607–1776

Chapter 5 Opener, page 119

○ Direct students' attention to the photo. Ask them what is happening in the photo.
○ Have students discuss the four questions. This can be done in pairs, in small groups, or as a class.
○ Check students' predictions of the chapter topic.

PART ① INTRODUCTION COLONIAL AMERICANS: WHO WERE THEY?, PAGES 120–123

Before Reading

CRITICAL THINKING STRATEGY: Thinking Ahead

○ Thinking ahead is an important critical thinking skill. It allows students to anticipate the content of readings, which in turn promotes comprehension.

Thinking Ahead

○ Have students look at the photos and read the questions.
○ Put students in pairs to answer the questions.
○ Call on students to share their ideas with the class.

ANSWER KEY

Answers will vary.

EXPANSION ACTIVITY: Impact Statements

○ Tell students that you will say the beginning of a sentence, and each student must complete the sentence quickly in turn. For example, if you say "One positive contribution immigrants have made to my culture is…" and point to a student, that student should complete the sentence (e.g., *great food*).

○ Continue around the room with other sentences (e.g., *One impact immigrants have had on my culture is…, One effect of colonists has been…, Countries that were colonized by European countries are…*).
○ In a variation, write the sentence starters on strips of paper. Call on a student to draw a strip and read it aloud. Have the student point to another student who will complete the sentence. Continue until everyone has had a chance to participate.

∩ Reading

○ Have students look at the reading. Go over the directions and the questions.
○ Have students read the passage silently, or have students follow along silently as you play the audio program.

Culture Notes:

○ You may want to point out that the focus of this reading is on colonists, or people who came from somewhere else to settle in this country. Of course, many people—Native Americans—were living in the area already.
○ Native American tribes in the area that would become the 13 colonies included the Huron, Algonquin, Iroquois, Seminole, Creek, Choctaw, Cherokee, and the Powhatan.

EXPANSION ACTIVITY: Native American Research

○ Put students in small groups to prepare a presentation.
○ Have students go online or to the library to research one of the Native American tribes living on the east coast of the United States in the 18th century (see culture note above for suggestions of tribes).

○ You may want to use the following questions as prompts: *Where did they live? How many were there in the tribe? What did they eat? What was their culture like?*
○ Have students present their research to the class.

After Reading

A. Check Your Understanding

○ Go over the directions.
○ Have students complete the chart.
○ Have students discuss their answers with a partner.
○ Go over the answers with the class.

ANSWER KEY

Who were they? Where did they come from?	Why did they come to the colonies?	What did they do in the colonies?
The English; England	They came for religious freedom.	They were farmers, blacksmiths, stonecutters, carpenters, doctors, lawyers, and religious leaders.
Other Europeans; Scotland, Germany, Holland, France, Sweden, Finland	They wanted a better, safer, and more peaceful life.	They were farmers, weavers, potters, and artists.
Africans; Africa	They were kidnapped and forced to work.	They were slaves.

B. Making Inferences

○ Go over the directions.
○ Put students in pairs to discuss and answer the questions.
○ Go over the answers with the class.

ANSWER KEY

Answers will vary, but may include these ideas:
- Life was probably difficult for some people in Europe, especially the poor or people who belonged to certain religious groups. Most people didn't own a lot of things, and they worked hard.
- Life was probably extremely difficult for Africans in the English colonies because almost all were slaves. They were forced to work very hard. They were not treated very nicely.

TOEFL® iBT Tip

TOEFL iBT Tip 1: The TOEFL iBT tests the ability to make inferences or draw conclusions based on what is implied in a passage.

○ Point out that the *Making Inferences* activity requires students to draw conclusions and form generalizations based on information presented in the reading.

○ By using key words and phrases from the text, students will be able to make assumptions and apply this skill to the reading section of the TOEFL iBT.

On the TOEFL iBT this question may appear in the format such as:
Which of the following can be inferred from paragraph ___ about _____?

C. Applying Information

○ Go over the directions.
○ Put students in small groups to answer the questions.
○ Call on students to share their ideas with the class.

ANSWER KEY

Answers will vary.

EXPANSION ACTIVITY: Name Game

○ Photocopy and distribute the Black Line Master *The Name Game* on page BLM 8.

○ Explain that many English last names come from a profession or another characteristic. Point out that sometimes the origin of the name isn't clear and they may have to make a guess. Point out it might be helpful to sound out the name.

○ Have students match the last name with its origin and then compare answers with a partner. Encourage students to try to figure out the unfamiliar words.

○ Go over the answers with the class.

○ For an additional challenge, assign each student a name from the list to research. Ask students to see if they can find someone famous with that name.

○ *Note:*
  - A cooper made barrels and wooden tubs, which were called cupes.
  - Chandler comes from the French word "chandelier," a lighting fixture that held candles in earlier times.
  - A mill is a building where grain is ground into flour.
  - A tailor is someone who makes clothes.

ANSWER KEY

1. t; 2. p; 3. f; 4. o; 5. s; 6. n; 7. r; 8. l; 9. a; 10. d; 11. q; 12. j; 13. k; 14. g; 15. m; 16. h; 17. b; 18. e; 19. c; 20. i

PART ❷ GENERAL INTEREST READING
FAMOUS COLONIAL AMERICANS, PAGES 124–129

Before Reading

A. Thinking Ahead

○ Go over the directions.

○ Put students in small groups to answer the questions.

○ Call on students to share their ideas with the class.

ANSWER KEY

Answers will vary. See ideas below.

1. Colonists had a difficult life, but they did have some comforts: education, books, music, better food and clothing. Slaves worked very hard and usually lived in very poor conditions.

2. Colonists, especially men, had quite a bit of freedom. Slaves had none.

3. Male colonists had some rights, but women couldn't vote. Slaves were treated as property, not people.

B. Previewing

○ Go over the directions.

○ Have students work in pairs to discuss Benjamin Franklin and Phillis Wheatley and answer the questions.

○ Go over the answers with the class.

ANSWER KEY

1. He probably did experiments with kites.
2. She probably wrote poems.

EXPANSION ACTIVITY: Why Are They Famous?

○ Put students in pairs or small groups.

○ Give students 30 seconds to write down a list of famous people in their country.

○ Elicit examples of famous people. Have students work in the same pairs or small groups to list the reasons the people they listed are famous.

○ Elicit reasons and write them on the board.

○ Ask students to discuss in their groups how the reasons for fame might be different now than they were in Colonial America, and why Benjamin Franklin and Phillis Wheatley might have been famous.

○ Call on students to share ideas.

READING STRATEGY: Guessing the Meanings of New Words: Using an Explanation in the Next Sentence

○ Go over the information in the box.

TOEFL® iBT Tip

TOEFL iBT Tip 2: The TOEFL iBT tests the ability to determine the meaning of words in context.

○ Point out that the activity *Guessing the Meanings of New Words* will help students improve their vocabulary for the TOEFL iBT. By identifying words that are used to define or explain other words and understanding their meanings, students will be able to apply this information toward further understanding the concepts presented in the text.

○ This skill may also be applied to insert text and cohesion type questions where students may determine how information in a paragraph is linked by looking at vocabulary words that are explained, defined, or used redundantly in a text.

On the TOEFL iBT this question appears in the following format:

The word_____ in the passage is closest in meaning to…

C. Guessing the Meanings of New Words
○ Go over the directions.

EXPANSION ACTIVITY: Skim the Reading
○ Write the following words on the board: *printer, autobiography, lightning rod, uniting*.
○ Have students skim the reading to find these words and the explanations that follow.
○ Go over the answers with the class.

ANSWER KEY
printer—published all kinds of things: newspapers, books, pamphlets
autobiography—the story of his own life
lightning rod—metal pole on the top of a building that attracts electricity and keeps the building and people inside it safe
uniting—join together

🎧 Reading
○ Go over the directions and the questions.
○ Have students read the passage silently, or have students follow along silently as you play the audio program.
○ Ask students what sentences they highlighted in the reading to answer the questions: *How were Benjamin Franklin and Phillis Wheatley different from each other? How were they similar to each other?*

ANSWER KEY
Highlighted from the reading:
– "one was a middle-class white man born in Boston, Massachusetts; the other was a female slave born in Senegal, Africa"
– "both were successful, creative individuals, and both had strong feelings about American independence"

After Reading

A. Check Your Understanding
○ Go over the directions.
○ Have students complete the chart.
○ Go over the answers with the class.

ANSWER KEY

	Benjamin Franklin	Phillis Wheatley
Born where?	Boston	Senegal, Africa
Born when?	1706	1753
Lived where?	Boston and Philadelphia	Boston and England
Died when?	1790	1784
Interests	Printing, writing, science, inventions, politics	Writing, poetry, politics, religion, slavery

(continued)

Accomplish-ments	Wrote autobiography; published *Poor Richard's Almanack,* books, and newspapers; invented lightning rod; helped write the Declaration of Independence	Learned to read and write; studied history, geography, and Latin; wrote first poem at age 13; wrote a book of poetry; met George Washington

EXPANSION ACTIVITY: Same or Different

○ Give students a few minutes to review the reading and their answers in Activity A.

○ After students have reviewed the material, tell students that you will dictate several words and phrases. Have students write down the phrases as you dictate. Next to each phrase, students should write *same* or *different,* to indicate if Franklin and Wheatley are the same or different in that regard.

○ Have students close their books. Dictate the following words and phrases: *birthplace, age at death, country of birth, greatest accomplishment, city lived in first, level of fame.*

○ Have students compare answers with a partner.

○ Go over answers with the class.

○ In an oral variation of this activity, call on students and say one of the phrases. Elicit if the two famous Americans are the same or different.

ANSWER KEY

birthplace: different; age at death: different; country of birth: different; greatest accomplishment: answers may vary, both wrote books; city in the longest: different; level of fame: answers may vary

CRITICAL THINKING STRATEGY: Using a Venn Diagram to Show Similarities and Differences

○ Go over the information in the box.

○ Ask: *What are two things that are the same for English immigrants and immigrants from other European countries? What is different about English immigrants? What is different about other Europeans?*

B. Using a Venn Diagram to Show Similarities and Differences

○ Go over the directions.

○ Have students work in pairs to complete the Venn diagram.

○ Go over the answers with the class.

ANSWER KEY

Answers should include:

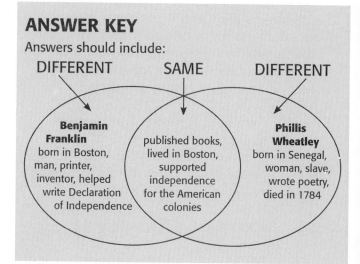

DIFFERENT   SAME   DIFFERENT

Benjamin Franklin
born in Boston, man, printer, inventor, helped write Declaration of Independence

published books, lived in Boston, supported independence for the American colonies

Phillis Wheatley
born in Senegal, woman, slave, wrote poetry, died in 1784

Academic Note:

○ Venn diagrams are used often in schools in the United States, particularly in mathematics. Make sure students understand that they should be used when comparing two things of the same class that have some similarities and some differences.

 ## C. Vocabulary Check

○ Go over the directions and the example.

○ Have students write the words on the lines.

○ Go over the answers.

ANSWER KEY

1. printing shop; 2. autobiography; 3. retired; 4. theory; 5. lightning rod; 6. uniting; 7. exception

D. Review: Understanding Pronouns
○ Go over the directions and the example.
○ Have students write the correct references on the lines.
○ Go over the answers with the class.

ANSWER KEY
1. poem; 2. Benjamin Franklin and Phillis Wheatley; 3. Franklin; 4. poem

---

EXPANSION ACTIVITY: Find Examples
○ Have students reread the passage to find three more examples of pronouns.
○ Have students copy the sentence containing the noun and the sentence containing the pronoun for each example, as was done in Activity D (e.g., *Later, Franklin moved to Philadelphia and started his own printing business. There, he published a newspaper.*).
○ Put students in pairs to exchange sentences. Have students underline the pronoun and circle the reference in their partner's sentences. Have students check their partner's answers.

E. Applying Your Knowledge
○ Remind students that applying knowledge is an important critical thinking skill.
○ Go over the directions.
○ Put students in small groups to discuss the questions.
○ Call on representatives from each group to tell the class about their group's ideas.

ANSWER KEY
Answers will vary.

PART ③ ACADEMIC READING: THE ROAD TO REBELLION, PAGES 130–136

Before Reading
A. Vocabulary Presentation
○ Go over the directions.
○ Have students circle the correct parts of speech for each word in red. Then have students guess the meanings of each word from the context and write their guesses on the lines.
○ Put students in pairs to compare answers, looking words up in the dictionary if their answers are different.
○ Go over the answers with the class.

ANSWER KEY
1. v; buy and sell goods; 2. v; take things into the country secretly; 3. v; speak or act against things they disagree with; 4. v; canceled; 5. n; things they are angry about

READING STRATEGY: Previewing: Scanning for Years
○ Go over the information in the box.
○ Ask: *What is scanning? Why should we scan for years?*

B. Scanning for Years
○ Go over the directions.
○ Have students scan for dates and write the dates on the lines.
○ Elicit the dates from students.

ANSWER KEY
1763, 1600s, 1766, 1767, 1773, 1774, 1776

READING STRATEGY: Previewing: Scanning for Events
○ Go over the information in the box.
○ Ask: *Why is scanning for events a good way to preview?*

C. Scanning for Events

- ○ Go over the directions.
- ○ Have students scan for the acts that the British government passed.
- ○ Elicit the events from students.

ANSWER KEY

Grenville Acts, Navigation Acts, Sugar Act, Stamp Act, Quartering Act, Townshend Acts, Tea Act, Intolerable Acts

TOEFL® iBT Tip

TOEFL iBT Tip 3: The TOEFL iBT tests the ability to understand key facts and important information contained within a text. Skimming and scanning to locate key information in a text will help students answer these types of questions.

- ○ Point out that the reading section of the TOEFL iBT may require examinees to identify information in the passage—events, dates, people, and other important information.

- ○ The activities, *Scanning for Years* and *Scanning for Events,* require students to identify specific information in a history text. Historically related topics are included on the test, and facts, dates, and events may be tested based on information from the reading.

- ○ Mastering this skill can help to scaffold students' abilities upward toward mastering the fact question on the test.

On the TOEFL iBT this question may appear in the format such as:
  According to the passage, {X} is…

EXPANSION ACTIVITY: More Practice

- ○ Have students scan and write down dates from the reading *Famous Colonial Americans.*
- ○ Have students write the events next to each date.

ANSWER KEY

1706—Franklin born; 1751—Franklin joins Pennsylvania Assembly; 1776—Franklin helps write Declaration of Independence; 1775–1783—the War for Independence; 1790—Franklin died; 1753—Wheatley born; 1761—Wheatley bought as slave; 1773—Wheatley gets freedom; 1776—Wheatley writes poem to George Washington

D. Thinking Ahead

- ○ Go over the directions.
- ○ Put students in pairs to discuss the questions.
- ○ Call on students to share their ideas with the class.

ANSWER KEY

Answers will vary.

🎧 Reading

- ○ Go over the directions and the question. Point out that students will answer this question in Activity A after the reading.
- ○ Have students read the passage silently, or play the audio program and have students follow along silently.

EXPANSION ACTIVITY: Key Ideas

- ○ Explain that one way to remember more from a reading is to keep track of the main ideas. Although every reading has one main idea that unites the entire reading, each paragraph can also have a main idea and topic.
- ○ To help students identify the topic in a paragraph, suggest they answer the question: *What is this paragraph about?*
- ○ As students read the passage, have them write down a topic or key idea next to each paragraph.
- ○ Put students in pairs to compare ideas.
- ○ Call on students to share their ideas with the class.

ANSWER KEY

paragraph 1—reasons for new laws; paragraph 2—1763 laws and taxes; paragraph 3—reasons for the Quartering Act; paragraph 4—taxation without representation; paragraph 5—acts of protest; paragraph 6—more tax laws and searches; paragraph 7—protest groups; paragraph 8—the Tea Act and boycott; paragraph 9—punishment for the Boston Tea Party; paragraph 10—reaction of colonists to the Intolerable Acts

After Reading

A. Main Idea

○ Review what a main idea is.
○ Go over the directions.
○ Have students discuss the questions in small groups.
○ Go over the answers with the class.

ANSWER KEY

The main reason that the American colonists wanted to be independent from Great Britain was they wanted representation—they wanted a say in the government if they were going to be taxed.

READING STRATEGY: Making a Timeline

○ Go over the information in the box.
○ Ask: *What do timelines show? What can they help you do?*

TOEFL® iBT Tip

TOEFL iBT Tip 4: The TOEFL iBT tests the ability to understand facts, examples, and explanations in a text; however, it does not directly test understanding of the main idea of a passage.

○ The *Making a Timeline* activity in Activity B and the following Expansion Activity require students to visually connect information in a chronological way. This will help to scaffold students' abilities upward toward mastering the schematic table questions on the test because it is a form of graphic organizer.

○ Remind students that being able to skim and scan to locate information is a technique that will help them with the schematic table question type on the test.

EXPANSION ACTIVITY: Your Timeline

○ Draw a line on the board.
○ Model the activity. Tell students about important events in your life and the years in which they happened (*I graduated high school in 1986.*). As you tell about the events, write them on the timeline next to the year.
○ Have students draw a timeline and indicate important events in their own lives.
○ Put students in pairs to talk about their timelines.
○ You can tape students' timelines on the walls of the room and have students walk around to look at them, or call on students to tell the class about some events on their timelines.

 ### B. Making a Timeline

○ Go over the directions.
○ Draw the timeline on the board.
○ Have students complete the timeline.
○ Have volunteers put the events on the timeline on the board.

ANSWER KEY

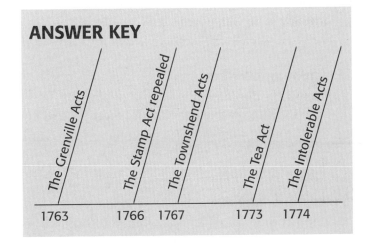

The Grenville Acts — 1763
The Stamp Act repealed — 1766
The Townshend Acts — 1767
The Tea Act — 1773
The Intolerable Acts — 1774

C. Understanding Details:

○ Go over the directions.
○ Have students match the acts with their descriptions.
○ Have students check their answers in the reading.
○ Go over the answers with the class.

ANSWER KEY

1. e; 2. a; 3. c; 4. b; 5. d

 ## D. Vocabulary Check

○ Go over the directions.
○ Have students write the correct words and phrases on the lines.
○ Go over the answers with the class.

ANSWER KEY

1. boycott; 2. writs of assistance; 3. Patriots; 4. Loyalists

Vocabulary Note:

○ The word *boycott* did not exist at the time of the Boston Tea Party. The word was coined in 1880, after an English land agent named Charles Boycott. Boycott collected rents in Ireland. The Irish decided to protest the high rents by refusing to have anything to do with Boycott at all.

E. Cause and Effect

○ Go over the directions.
○ Have students complete the graphic organizer and then compare answers with a partner.
○ Go over the answers with the class.

ANSWER KEY

British Actions	Colonists' Reactions
the Stamp Act ——————→	boycott
act repealed ←——————	
the Tea Act ——————→	the Boston Tea Party
the Intolerable Acts ←——→	idea of independence

CRITICAL THINKING STRATEGY: Making Connections

○ Remind students that making connections between ideas is an important critical thinking skill that can help them remember new information.

F. Making Connections

○ Go over the directions.
○ Put students in pairs to discuss and answer the question.
○ Call on students to share their ideas with the class.

ANSWER KEY

Answers will vary.

G. Application

○ Go over the directions.
○ Put students in small groups to answer the questions.
○ Call on students to share their ideas with the class.

ANSWER KEY

Answers will vary.

H. Word Journal

○ Go over the directions.
○ Have students write important words in their Word Journals.

I. Journal Writing

○ Go over the directions. Have students choose one of the topics.
○ Explain that this is a quick-writing activity and does not have to be perfect. Point out that journal writing can be a warm-up to a more structured writing assignment, helping to generate ideas.
○ Have students write. Set a time limit of 10 minutes.
○ Put students in pairs to read or talk about their writing.

Website Research

○ For additional information on the thirteen colonies:
- 13 Originals, Founding the Americans Colonies–The Time Page
  (http://www.timepage.org/spl/13colony.html)
- The Thirteen Colonies–Cave Spring Middle School
  (http://www.rcs.k12.va.us/csjh/colonies.htm)
- 13 Original Colonies–Wentworth Intermediate School
  (http://www.scarborough.k12.me.us/wis/teachers/dtewhey/webquest/colonial/13_original_colonies.htm)

○ For additional information on famous American colonists and life in the colonies:
- Archiving Early America
  (http://www.earlyamerica.com)
- Colonial Williamsburg–Explore & Learn
  (http://www.history.org/history)
- Webography, Settlement of British America–Colonial Williamsburg
  (http://research.history.org/JDRLibrary/Online_Resources/Research_Topics/WebSettlement.cfm)

PART ④ THE MECHANICS OF WRITING, PAGES 137–141

○ Go over the directions.

A. Review: Simple Past

○ Go over the directions.
○ Have students write five sentences about an event or famous person in history using the simple past and the verbs in the box. Remind students to use at least two negatives.
○ Call on students to read sentences to the class.

ANSWER KEY
Answers will vary.

Can and *Could*

○ Go over the information in the box.
○ Ask: *What form of the verb follows* can *and* could? *Which do we use to talk about ability in the past? What is something you can do now that you couldn't do 10 years ago?*

B. *Can* and *Could*

○ Go over the directions.
○ Have students write four sentences using *can* and *could* and then compare sentences with a partner.
○ Call on students to read sentences to the class.

ANSWER KEY
Answers will vary.

EXPANSION ACTIVITY: Who Am I?

○ Model the activity. Say several sentences about yourself in which you contrast your abilities in the past and now using *can* and *could* (e.g., *When I was 13, I couldn't speak French, but now I can.*).
○ Have students write five sentences on a piece of paper in which they contrast their abilities in the past and present using *can* and *could*. Encourage students to write sentences that are about their own individual abilities, rather than sentences that are true for most people (e.g., *When I was 6, I couldn't drive a car* is a sentence that is true for most people.).
○ Collect the papers.
○ Read the sentences aloud to the class and have students guess who wrote the sentences.

Causatives: *Force* and *Make*

○ Go over the information in the box.
○ Ask: *When do we use causatives? What form of the verb can follow* force? *What form can follow* make?

C. Causatives

○ Go over the directions and the example.
○ Have students write sentences using the cues and then compare answers with a partner.
○ Go over the answers with the class.

ANSWER KEY

1. England forced the colonists to buy English tea.
2. Great Britain made the colonists pay a tax on newspapers.
3. The Sugar Act forced the Americans to pay a tax on sugar.
4. English laws made the colonists want independence.
5. A Virginia law forced African servants to become slaves.

TEST-TAKING STRATEGY: Paraphrasing

○ Go over the information in the box.
○ Ask: *What is paraphrasing? What are some ways to paraphrase?*

D. Paraphrasing

○ Go over the directions and the example.
○ Have students paraphrase the sentences.
○ Call on students to share their ideas with the class.

ANSWER KEY

Answers will vary. See ideas below.
1. Many Europeans settled in America because they wanted the freedom to practice religion their own way.
2. Some people came from Europe because they wanted peace, food, and to be treated fairly.
3. Traders forced many people from Africa to become slaves in America.
4. Many colonists were religious.
5. Europeans owned African slaves.

TOEFL® iBT Tip

TOEFL iBT Tip 5: The TOEFL iBT tests the ability to read a passage, listen to a lecture related to that passage, and then write in response to a question based on the two stimuli. This integrated writing skill requires students to think critically about material that they have read, interpret that information and relate it to a lecture, and then present ideas in essay format.

○ Remind students that paraphrasing is an important skill to develop. When listening to a lecture and taking notes, or reading a passage and taking notes, students must be able to then paraphrase and cite the information they wish to analyze.

○ In the integrated writing section of the test, students are encouraged to refer to information from the text or lecture. Excellent note-taking and paraphrasing of spoken and written information will help students improve their overall writing skills for the test.

Summary Writing: Condensing

○ Go over the information in the box.
○ Ask: *What do you keep when you write a summary? What does it mean to condense? What can you leave out when you condense? What should you use in a summary to connect ideas?*

E. Condensing

○ Go over the directions.
○ Have students write new sentences on the lines that condense the material.
○ Put students in pairs to compare sentences.
○ Call on students to read sentences to the class.

ANSWER KEY

Answers will vary. See ideas below.

1. In the colonies, most white settlers were farmers or merchants.
2. Many people who came to the English colonies came as indentured servants.
3. For fun, people told stories, read aloud, played games, or sang songs.
4. Many people could not pay their way to America, so they became indentured servants to repay their master.
5. Female colonists, like English women, could not vote or own property. They worked hard, especially on farms.

EXPANSION ACTIVITY: Pair Exchange

○ Have students select one of the paragraphs that they have written for the writing assignments in Chapters 1–4.
○ Put students in pairs to exchange paragraphs.
○ Have students condense their partner's paragraph. Encourage students to reduce it to one or two sentences.
○ Have students share the condensed version with their partners.
○ Call on students to tell the class what they learned from the condensing activity.

F. Review/Editing

○ Go over the directions.
○ Have students find and correct the mistakes and then compare answers with a partner.
○ Go over the answers with the class.

ANSWER KEY

Most Africans in North America ~~was~~ ∧*were* slaves. They live∧*d* on plantations. They ~~have~~ ∧*had* very hard lives. Some Africans did housework, but most work∧*ed* in the fields.

The large plantation owners hired overseers, or bosses.

The overseers made the slaves ~~to~~ work hard. There were many rules for slaves. Slaves ~~cannot~~ ∧*could not* leave the plantation without permission from their master (owner). They ~~cannot~~ ∧*could not* learn to read or write.

PART 5 ACADEMIC WRITING, PAGES 142–143

Writing Assignment

○ Go over the writing assignment.
○ Have students read the five steps.
○ Direct students' attention to Step A and have students choose a reading from this chapter to summarize.

WRITING STRATEGY: Writing a Summary

○ Go over the information in the box.
○ Ask comprehension questions such as: *What are characteristics of a summary? If there are 12 paragraphs, how many sentences should you write? What do you say in the topic sentence? Can you add new information in a summary? Can you leave anything out?*
○ Direct students' attention to the example. Ask: *What is some information in the reading that is not included in the summary?*

○ Direct students' attention to Step B. Have students answer the questions using short notes.
○ Direct students' attention to Step C. Have students write paragraphs, using their notes from Step B. Remind students to follow the rules in the bullets in the Writing Strategy box.
○ Direct students' attention to Step D. Have students read and edit their paragraphs, looking for mistakes in paragraph form, the topic sentence, tenses, *can* and *could*, causitives, paraphrasing and condensing.
○ To encourage peer editing, have students exchange paragraphs with a partner, edit, and return to the writer.
○ Direct students' attention to Step E. Have students rewrite the paragraphs.
○ Collect the paragraphs.

TOEFL® iBT Tip

TOEFL iBT Tip 6: The TOEFL iBT writing section requires examinees to summarize major points and important details from sources. This is more evident in integrated tasks, but this skill can also be applied to independent writing tasks.

○ Point out to students that the strategies in this chapter (vocabulary, reference, main idea, details, inference, and paraphrasing skills) will help them to interpret what they hear and read and to then write about the topic *in their own words*.

○ Generally, students will have 20 minutes to plan and write a response to an integrated writing task.

On the TOEFL iBT this question may appear in the following format:

Summarize the points made in the lecture you just heard, explaining how they compare to (or cast doubt on, refute) points made in the reading. You may refer to the reading passage as you write.

EXPANSION ACTIVITY: Editing Practice

○ Photocopy and distribute the Black Line Master *Editing Practice* on page BLM 9.
○ Go over the directions.
○ Have students correct the mistakes and then compare answers with a partner.
○ Go over the answers with the class.

ANSWER KEY

Many poor people in England ~~come~~ *came* to the colonies as indentured servants. Unemployment ~~were~~ *was* high, and they ~~can't~~ *couldn't* work in Great Britain. They signed a contract in England and agree*d* to work for a period of four to seven years. In exchange, they receive*d* their trip over for free and clothes, food, and shelter in the New World. However, the indentured servants were surprised at their new lives. Their masters often forced them *to* work in the fields, instead of in their former professions. These servants ~~cannot~~ *could not* marry or have children. Their masters ~~can~~ *could* sell their contract to someone else. The masters often ~~maked~~ *made* the servants ~~to~~ live in poor conditions. Many died before they got their freedom.

UNIT 3

U.S. HISTORY

CHAPTER 6 A CHANGING NATION: 1850–1900

In this chapter, students will learn about American history between 1850 and 1900. In the first section, students will read quotes from Native Americans, settlers, and immigrants as they migrated to and lived in the West. In Part 2, students will learn about the settlement of the frontier and the loss of the Native American way of life. Finally, students will read about changing patterns of immigration and the countries the new immigrants came from. These topics will prepare students to write a paragraph about American life in the second half of the nineteenth century.

VOCABULARY

buffalo	homesteaders	ranches
cattle drives	hostility	resent
crops	journey	reservations
droughts	miners	scapegoats
famine	newcomers	settlers
frontier	the plains	train track
ghost towns	railroad	treaties

READING STRATEGIES
Interpreting Graphs
Finding Specific Support
Understanding Cause and Effect

CRITICAL THINKING STRATEGIES
Thinking Ahead (Part 1)
Making Connections (Part 1)
Using a T-Chart (Part 3)
Note: Strategy in bold is highlighted in the student book.

MECHANICS
Transition Words of Contrast
Using *There + Be*
Using Quotations to Support General Statements

TEST-TAKING STRATEGY
Finding Unstated Details

WRITING STRATEGY
Writing a Paragraph of Comparison

CHAPTER 6 A Changing Nation 1850–1900

Chapter 6 Opener, page 145

○ Direct students' attention to the photo. Ask them what is happening in the photo.
○ Have students discuss the four questions. This can be done in pairs, in small groups, or as a class.
○ Check students' predictions of the chapter topic.

PART ① INTRODUCTION VOICES FROM THE PAST, PAGES 146–149

Before Reading

• •

CRITICAL THINKING STRATEGY: Thinking Ahead

○ Thinking ahead is an important critical thinking strategy. It allows students to anticipate the content of readings, which in turn promotes comprehension.

• •

Thinking Ahead

○ Have students look at the photos and read the questions.
○ Put students in pairs to answer the questions.
○ Call on students to share their ideas with the class.

ANSWER KEY

Answers will vary.

EXPANSION ACTIVITY: What Do You Know?

○ Ask students where they have heard about the Old West or "Wild West" before (e.g., *books, classes, movies, TV shows*).
○ Put students in pairs or small groups to brainstorm everything they know or associate with the Old West in the United States.

○ Elicit ideas from students and write them on the board.
○ As students read the quotes in Part 1, ask students to notice if their impressions are reinforced or contradicted by the actual words of the people who lived during that time.

🎧 Reading

○ Have students look at the reading. Ask: *What kind of reading is this? How many different "writers" are there?* Go over the directions and the question.
○ Have students read the passage silently, or have students follow along silently as you play the audio program.
○ Elicit ideas from students about what they can learn about American history from the quotes.
○ If students did the expansion activity *What Do You Know?*, ask students if their impressions from the expansion activity were confirmed by the information in the quotes.

Culture Notes:

○ Nicolas Stott Shaw was an early pioneer woman.
○ Red Cloud was a warrior and statesman for the Lakota Sioux, a tribe living in the Great Plains. In 1866, Red Cloud led a successful war against the United States, but in 1874, the Indians were defeated. He continued to fight for the well-being of his people through the 1880s.
○ Chief Joseph led a tribe from Oregon who resisted moving to a small reservation. He and his tribe became famous for a three-month march, during which a small band of warriors fought a couple thousand U.S. soldiers.
○ Carl Schurz was the U.S. Secretary of the Interior under President Rutherford Hayes. He was born in Germany and immigrated to the United States, where he became a newspaperman and an army officer. He was opposed to slavery and fought for the Union Army during the Civil War.
○ Mary Antin was a Jewish writer born in Russia. Her family fled religious persecution in Russia.

○ W.E.B. Du Bois was an African American, born in 1868. He studied at Harvard and then in Germany, where he became very interested in the problems of race. He worked throughout his life to help African Americans and to deal with racial problems.

After Reading

A. Making Inferences
○ Go over the directions.
○ Have students write their answers in the chart.
○ Have students discuss their answers with a partner.
○ Go over the answers with the class.

ANSWER KEY
1. Red Cloud, Chief Joseph, Carl Schurz
2. resident of Newton
3. Nicolas Stott Shaw
4. Carl Schurz
5. Scandinavian immigrant, Mary Antin
6. Red Cloud, Chief Joseph, Carl Schurz
7. Scandinavian immigrant

EXPANSION ACTIVITY: True or False
○ Divide the class into two or more teams.
○ Have each team write true and false statements based on the quotes in the reading. Encourage students to make inferences in addition to references to directly stated information.
○ Give students five minutes to review the quotes.
○ Have the teams take turns challenging each other by reading a statement and eliciting if it is true or false. The responding team must say what information in the quotes supports the answer.

READING STRATEGY: Interpreting Graphs
○ Go over the information in the box.
○ Ask: *What kind of information can you find in graphs? How do graphs differ from text? How can graphs help you understand information?*

B. Comparing Graphs About Population Change
○ Go over the directions.
○ Put students in pairs to answer the questions.
○ Go over the answers with the class.

ANSWER KEY
1. The total population increased.
2. The Native American population decreased.
3. Answers will vary. Possible ideas include: the immigrants killed the Native Americans, the Native Americans had less food because the settlers took so much land, the settlers took the food, the settlers/immigrants brought diseases to the Native Americans.

CRITICAL THINKING STRATEGY: Making Connections
○ Making connections is an important critical thinking strategy. It allows students to understand and remember new information by connecting it to something else.

C. Making Connections
○ Go over the directions.
○ Have students form small groups to discuss which quotations and photos might belong together. Point out that there may be more than one correct answer.
○ Go over the answers with the class.

ANSWER KEY
Answers may vary. Possible matches include:
Native-American village: Red Cloud, Chief Joseph, Carl Schurz
"Wild West" town: resident of Newton
Neighborhood of immigrants: Mary Antin, Scandinavian immigrant

TOEFL® iBT Tip

TOEFL iBT Tip 1: The TOEFL iBT tests the ability to understand key facts and the important information contained within a text. Locating key words in a text will help students build vocabulary and improve their reading skills.

○ Point out that students will benefit from doing the *Making Connections* activity that focuses on making connections between ideas in order to prepare for the classification/matching details question type.

○ This activity requires students to connect and organize information. It will help to scaffold students' abilities upward toward mastering the schematic table questions on the test.

EXPANSION ACTIVITY: Sketch It

○ Explain that one way to remember new information is to create a visual image to associate with it. Point out that the image can be a complete drawing, or just a doodle or symbol.
○ Have students draw an image next to each quote.
○ Put students in pairs to talk about their images.
○ Call on students to tell the class about one of their images.

PART ② GENERAL INTEREST READING
THE END OF THE FRONTIER, PAGES 150–155

Before Reading

A. Discussion
○ Go over the directions.
○ Put students in small groups to answer the questions.
○ Call on students to share their ideas with the class.

ANSWER KEY

Answers may vary. See ideas below.
1. Miners work in mines, usually underground, digging for gold.
2. Problems might include: weather (drought, floods, snow), insects, diseases affecting crops or animals.
3. Their lives depended on the buffalo. Uses of buffalo: food, clothing, shelter, weapons.

B. Thinking Ahead
○ Go over the directions.
○ Have students write ideas in the chart and then discuss their ideas in small groups.
○ Call on students to share their ideas with the class.

ANSWER KEY
Answers will vary.

EXPANSION ACTIVITY: Before and After

○ Put students in pairs or small groups to discuss these questions: *How did things change in your country because of new forms of transportation? How is life in your native country impacted by transportation today? How are lifestyles affected (both positively and negatively)?*
○ Call on students to share their ideas with the class.

C. Vocabulary Preparation
○ Go over the directions.
○ Have students write the meaning of each new word on the line.
○ Go over the answers with the class.

ANSWER KEY
1. A journey is a trip, often in search of something.
2. Settlers are people who live in a new place and start farms or businesses.
3. Ranches are places where people raise cattle.
4. Droughts are times when there is no rain.
5. Examples of crops are corn and wheat.

D. Previewing
○ Go over the directions.
○ Have students write the two headings on the lines.
○ Elicit the headings.

ANSWER KEY

The Coming of the Railroad, The End of the Native Americans' Way of Life

EXPANSION ACTIVITY: Make Connections
○ Have students write three ideas for how the two headings might be connected.
○ Put students in pairs to compare ideas.
○ Call on students to share their ideas with the class.

🎧 Reading
○ Go over the directions and the question.
○ Have students read the passage silently, or have students follow along silently as you play the audio program.
○ Ask students what sentences they highlighted in the reading to answer the question: *How did the railroad change the western part of the United States?*

Culture Notes:
○ In 1847, a man named James Marshall discovered gold in California. Word spread, and soon thousands of people headed west. They were called "forty-niners" because most of them came in 1849.
○ In 1862, Congress authorized the Union Pacific and Central Pacific companies to begin building the first transcontinental railroad. They celebrated this joining by driving a golden spike (a very large nail) into the ground.

After Reading
A. Check Your Understanding
○ Go over the directions.
○ Have students answer the questions and then compare answers with a partner.
○ Go over the answers with the class.

ANSWER KEY

1. People could move west then because that is when the railroads were joined from the east to the west.
2. Reasons people wanted to move west included land, freedom, gold, and adventure.
3. The railroad changed the western part of the United States because it brought many people west to be miners, ranchers, and farmers. The new people wanted lots of land, and the Native Americans were forced to live on reservations.

🌏 B. Vocabulary Check
○ Go over the directions.
○ Have students highlight the words in the reading and then write the words on the lines next to the definitions.
○ Go over the answers with the class.

ANSWER KEY

1. frontier; 2. train track; 3. ghost towns; 4. cattle drives; 5. homesteaders; 6. Great Plains; 7. treaties; 8. reservation

TEST-TAKING STRATEGY: Finding Unstated Details
○ Go over the information in the box. Ask: *How do we find the correct answer for this kind of test question?*

TOEFL® iBT Tip

TOEFL iBT Tip 2: The TOEFL iBT tests the ability to understand key facts and the important information contained within a text. Using the strategy *Finding Unstated Details* in a text will help students build vocabulary and improve their reading skills.

○ Point out that the reading section of the TOEFL iBT may require examinees to identify information that is NOT included in the passage.

○ The *Finding Unstated Details* strategy and Activity C will help to scaffold students' abilities upward toward mastering the negative fact question on the test.

On the TOEFL iBT this question may appear in the format such as:

All of the following are mentioned in paragraph ___ as _____ EXCEPT...

C. Finding Details
○ Go over the directions.
○ Have students fill in the correct bubbles.
○ Go over the answers with the class.

ANSWER KEY
1. D; 2. B; 3. C; 4. A; 5. B

EXPANSION ACTIVITY: Two Yeses and a No
○ Give students two index cards. Have students write *yes* on one card and *no* on the other.
○ Have students write three sentences: Two sentences will include information that was in the passage, and one sentence will mention something not in the reading but on the same topic. Point out that this third sentence could be true or false—the important thing is that it is not addressed in the passage.

○ Call on students to read their three sentences to the class in random order. Instruct the other students to hold up the *yes* card after each sentence that contains information from the passage, and the *no* card after each sentence that is not about the reading. Encourage students to look around and self-correct.
○ Discuss the sentences about which students disagree.

READING STRATEGY: Finding Specific Support
○ Go over the information in the box.
○ Ask: *What do we mean by specific information? Where can you often find it?*

D. Finding Specific Support
○ Go over the directions.
○ Have students write the information on the lines.
○ Call on students to share their ideas with the class.

ANSWER KEY
1. sometimes ten miles of track in just one day
2. they did the work by hand, in terrible desert heat or in heavy snow
3. in summer, temperatures were over 100 degrees F; in winter, there was a lot of snow; they had droughts, insects, and it was lonely
4. buffalo meat was important in the Native American diet; buffalo skin was necessary for clothing, shoes, and housing; buffalo bones were good for tools and weapons

PART ③ ACADEMIC READING: CHANGING PATTERNS OF IMMIGRATION, PAGES 156–163

Before Reading

A. Vocabulary Preparation

○ Go over the directions.
○ Have students circle the correct part of speech then guess the meaning of each word from context and write it on the line.
○ Call on students to share ideas with the class.
○ Have students look up the dictionary definitions and write them on the lines.

ANSWER KEY

Answers will vary for guesses.
1. n; Dictionary Definition: a recent arrival
2. n; Dictionary Definition: a drastic food shortage, starvation
3. v; Dictionary Definition: to be angry and upset about something
4. n; Dictionary Definition: unfriendly and angry feelings or behavior

B. Previewing

○ Go over the directions.
○ Have students write the two headings on the lines and then compare answers with a partner.
○ Go over the answers with the class.

ANSWER KEY

The "Old Immigration," The "New Immigration"

EXPANSION ACTIVITY: Predict

○ Put students in pairs.
○ Give students one minute to brainstorm ways in which immigration to the United States might have changed between the 18th century and the end of the 19th century.
○ Call on students to share their ideas with the class.

C. Scanning for Specific Information

○ Go over the directions. Review what scanning is (to look quickly for specific information—in this case, the names of countries).
○ Have students scan the reading to find the names of countries and write them on the lines. Point out that in some cases, they may find the nationality and have to figure out the country.
○ Go over the answers with the class.

ANSWER KEY

Ireland, Germany, China, Italy, Russia, Poland, Austro-Hungarian Empire

---

Culture Notes:

○ The Austro-Hungarian Empire was formed in 1867 and included the countries of Austria and Hungary. It lasted until World War I, when it was divided into separate countries.

D. Thinking Ahead

○ Go over the directions.
○ Put students in small groups to discuss the questions.
○ Call on students to share their ideas with the class.

ANSWER KEY

Answers will vary.

🎧 Reading

○ Go over the directions and the question. Have students read the passage silently, or play the audio program and have students follow along silently.
○ Have students highlight phrases that answer the question as they find them in the reading.
○ When students have finished reading, ask what they highlighted.

ANSWER KEY

Answers may vary. Possibilities include the following:
- Many people began to come from southern and eastern Europe.
- The new immigrants moved to cities and lived together in their own neighborhoods. The old immigrants moved west to farms, midwest cities and mining towns.
- The new immigrants built churches, synagogues, clubs and started newspapers like home.

After Reading

CRITICAL THINKING STRATEGY: Using a T-Chart

○ Go over the information in the box. Ask: *When can you use a T-chart?*

A. Check Your Understanding

○ Go over the directions.
○ Have students complete the T-chart and then compare answers with a partner.
○ Go over the answers with the class.

ANSWER KEY

	Old Immigration	New Immigration
1. When did this period start?	1830s	1865
2. Where did the people come from?	Ireland, Germany, China	southern and eastern Europe: Italy, Russia, Poland, Austro-Hungarian Empire
3. Where did the immigrants settle?	New York, Boston, Midwest, and Pacific coast	cities like New York, stayed in own neighborhoods
4. What were the Americans' attitudes toward the newcomers?	beginning of resentment and anger	more serious resentment, hostility

EXPANSION ACTIVITY: More Practice

○ Have students create a T-chart to compare the lives of settlers and Native Americans. Remind students to review the first two readings to get ideas.
○ Put students in pairs to compare charts.
○ Call on students to share their ideas with the class.

ANSWER KEY

Answers will vary. See ideas below.

Settlers	Native Americans
numbers of settlers growing	number of Native Americans decreasing
hope of a better life	feeling sad
getting land	losing land
killed buffalo for sport	used buffalo for food, shelter, clothing, tools, weapons

 B. Pronoun Reference

○ Go over the directions.
○ Have students highlight the noun or noun phrase the pronoun refers to.
○ Go over the answers with the class.

ANSWER KEY

1. Highlight: some native-born Americans
2. Highlight: These new immigrants
3. Highlight: The old resentment

READING STRATEGY: Understanding Cause and Effect

❍ Go over the information in the box.
❍ Point out that *because* is used with a clause (*because I was late*), and *because of* is used before a noun (*because of the weather*).
❍ Ask: *What is an expression that is similar to because? What two expressions mean that's why?*

TOEFL® iBT Tip

TOEFL iBT Tip 3: The TOEFL iBT may require students to determine the author's rhetorical purpose of a text. This type of question measures the ability to determine why an author uses a particular feature or example in a text.

❍ Mention to students that being familiar with cause-effect transition words may help them to recognize reasons and examples stated in a text.

❍ Remind students that recognizing these transition words can be applied to the answer choices of a rhetorical purpose question and further be applied to writing tasks on the test.

On the TOEFL iBT this question may appear in the format such as:
Why does the author introduce the claim...?

EXPANSION ACTIVITY: Graphic Organizer

❍ Photocopy and distribute the Black Line Master *Understanding Cause and Effect* on page BLM 10.
❍ Point out that students will have to make connections between the ideas in the readings in Parts 2 and 3 to complete the organizer.
❍ Have students complete the two cause and effect chains and then compare ideas with a partner.
❍ Go over the answers with the class.

ANSWER KEY

1. potato crop failure in Ireland → people immigrating from Ireland to the U.S. → many Irish immigrants worked on the railroad → railroad completed in 1869 → many more people moved west → Native Americans lost land and moved to reservations
2. poverty and persecution in home countries → immigration from southern and eastern Europe → A. moved to cities, stayed in neighborhoods, kept old customs B. got jobs that kept wages low → hostility towards new immigrants

C. Finding Reasons

❍ Go over the directions.
❍ Have students answer the questions. Remind students to refer to the passage.
❍ Go over the answers with the class.

ANSWER KEY

1. There was a famine because the potato crop failed;
2. They came to America because of crop failures, to escape persecution, or for religious freedom;
3. Workers were needed in the colonies; 4. They dressed and sounded different, and had strange religions; 5. They lived in their own neighborhoods and kept the dress and customs of the "old country"

TOEFL® iBT Tip

TOEFL iBT Tip 4: The TOEFL iBT requires examinees to recognize the minor, less important ideas that do not belong in a summary; or, distinguish between major and minor points of information.

❍ Point out that the activity *Finding Reasons* will help students distinguish between major and minor points in a text on the TOEFL iBT.

❍ Explain to students that this type of question is called a *prose summary* or *classification* question, and partial credit will be given for correct answers. On the TOEFL iBT, the answers to this type of question are not in traditional multiple-choice format.

○ Students will also benefit from doing the *Making Comparisons* activity in Activity D in order to prepare for the classification or prose summary question type.

This question type appears in the form of a schematic table that requires examinees to select and drag answer choices to specific positions in a chart.

EXPANSION ACTIVITY: *Why* Questions

○ Point out that we often use the expressions in the reading strategy *Understanding Cause and Effect* in answering *why* questions (*because, because of, due to, so,* and *therefore*).

○ Have students write three *why* questions based on the readings in this chapter.

○ Call on a student and ask a *why* question (e.g., *Why was life hard for the Indians?*). Remind the student to use one of the expressions in their answer.

○ Have the student call on a classmate and ask a *why* question and have the second student answer.

○ Continue until everyone has had a chance to participate.

D. Making Comparisons

○ Go over the directions.
○ Have students answer the questions in small groups.
○ Have students make T-charts for each pair of pictures.
○ Call on students to share their ideas with the class.

ANSWER KEY

Answers will vary. See ideas below.

The Hatch Family	A working class family
Similarities:	
big family	big family
Differences:	
wealthy	poor
large house with art	small, dark apartment
expensive carpets and curtains	laundry hanging above the stove
beautiful, clean clothes	shabby clothes
lived in comfort	life was difficult

Wedding of the Rails	*The Song of the Talking Wire*, painting
Differences:	
many people, celebrating, happy	one person, alone, seems unhappy
sunny, warm day	cold winter day
people wear city clothing (hats, pants, suits)	man wears traditional Native American clothing
can see manmade machines	can see natural environment, horses

Tom Torlino (Navajo Indian)	Tom Torlino in a white school
Similarities:	
Same pose	Same pose
not smiling	not smiling
Differences:	
Long hair	Short hair
Jewelry	No jewelry
Native dress	European style clothing (suit)

E. Word Journal

○ Go over the directions.
○ Have students write important words in their Word Journals.

F. Journal Writing

○ Go over the directions.
○ Explain that this is a quick-writing activity and does not have to be perfect. Point out that journal writing can be a warm-up to a more structured writing assignment, helping to generate ideas.
○ Have students write. Set a time limit of 10 minutes.
○ Put students in pairs to read or talk about their writing.

Website Research

❍ For additional information on immigration in the 19th century:
  • The Great Immigration Seneca Village Columbia University–Institute For Learning Technologies (http://projects.ilt.columbia.edu/Seneca/ AfAMNYC/06aAfAmNYC.html)
  • European Immigrants Leave Mark on Continent–The Brown Quarterly Volume 4 (http://brownvboard.org/brwnqurt/04-1/ 04-1b.htm)
  • Immigration and the cities in the 19th and 20th Centuries–Henry J. Sage (http://www.sagehistory.net/gildedage/ immigration.htm)
❍ For additional information on the westward migration:
  • Western Immigration–David G. Vanderstel (http://www.connerprairie.org/HistoryOnline/ migrate.html)
  • New Perspectives on the West–Pbs.Org, Episode Index (http://www.pbs.org/weta/thewest/program/ episodes/index.htm)
  • Immigration 19th Century, Perceptions–Library Of Congress (http://memory.loc.gov/learn/features/immig/ alt/native_american4.html)

PART ④ THE MECHANICS OF WRITING, ## PAGES 164–168

❍ Go over the directions.

Transition Words of Contrast

❍ Go over the information in the box about transition words of contrast.
❍ Ask: *What expressions can we use to express contrast? How is* in contrast *different from* but? Note that *but* is used to show all kinds of differences but *in contrast* is used only for big differences or opposites.

A. Sentence Combining

❍ Go over the directions.
❍ Have students combine the sentences.
❍ Call on students to read their sentences to the class.

ANSWER KEY

1. The railroad made it possible for many thousands of people to move west, but it also made it possible for them to take Native American land. *OR* The railroad made it possible for many thousands of people to move west. However, it also made it possible for them to take Native American land.
2. Many people hoped to get rich in the gold and silver mines, but very few were successful. *OR* Many people hoped to get rich in the gold and silver mines. However, very few were successful.
3. Mining towns were very busy places for a few years, but most of them are now ghost towns. *OR* Mining towns were very busy places for a few years. However, most of them are now ghost towns.
4. Some people became rich by mining, but Levi Strauss became rich by selling jeans to the miners. *OR* Some people became rich by mining. However/In contrast, Levi Strauss became rich by selling jeans to the miners.

Using *There + Be*

❍ Go over the information in the box. Point out that we often use *there + be* to describe situations.
❍ Ask: *What does the verb* be *agree with?*

EXPANSION ACTIVITY: Picture Description

❍ Have students choose a picture from this chapter.
❍ Have students write three sentences about the picture using *there + be*.
❍ Put students in pairs to exchange sentences. Have students identify the picture described in their partners' sentences.

B. Using *There + Be*

❍ Go over the directions.
❍ Have students complete the passage with the simple past tense form of the verbs in parentheses.
❍ Go over the answers with the class.

ANSWER KEY

1. came; 2. grew; 3. were; 4. was; 5. were; 6. wasn't;
7. crowded; 8. piled; 9. spread; 10. threw; 11. filled;
12. were; 13. weren't; 14. worked; 15. were; 16. were;
17. spent; 18. didn't go; 19. opened; 20. offered;
21. were; 22. wrote; 23. shocked; 24. began; 25. took;
26. became

Using Quotations to Support General Statements

❍ Go over the information in the box.
❍ Ask: *Why do we sometimes include quotations in our writing? What are three things you must remember to do when you use a quotation? What are some ways to introduce a quotation?*

C. Using Quotations

❍ Go over the directions.
❍ Have students read the quotations and then use the quotations to support the statements. Remind students to use one of the ways suggested on page 166 to introduce the quote.
❍ Put students in pairs to compare ideas.
❍ Go over the answers with the class.

ANSWER KEY

Answers may vary. See ideas below.
1. As one cowboy said, "There was a lot of dust and dirt, hard work and worry, and never enough sleep. Mostly it was damn boring."
2. One farmer noted, "I've never seen so many insects, so little rain, so much trouble and death in my life."
3. As Lame Horse, a Sioux Indian said, "They killed my family, my tribe. They took our land and left us nothing."
4. According to "Johnny" Wu, a railroad worker, "We worked in snow and heat, mountains and desert, sometimes 15 hours a day. We built every inch of that track by hand."
5. As Brigit O'Connor, an immigrant from Ireland, said, "In America we wouldn't be under someone's boot. We would work hard but get a fair wage, enough food, and maybe have a good life someday."

TOEFL® iBT Tip

TOEFL iBT Tip 5: Although the TOEFL iBT does not discretely test grammar skills, examinees' essay scores will be determined based on the range of grammar and vocabulary used in their essays.

❍ Point out that the grammar activities in *The Mechanics of Writing* part of this chapter will help them improve their use of verb tenses for essay writing.

❍ Point out that the activity *Using Quotations* will help students to improve their abilities to paraphrase and cite material from the listening and reading sources used for the integrated writing tasks.

❍ Students should be advised to make careful notes when listening to lectures or reading texts, but they should also make sure to quote from the sources accurately, as that is considered to be criteria for scoring the essay.

D. Review/Editing

○ Go over the directions.
○ Have students find and correct the mistakes and then compare answers with a partner. Tell students there might be a famous person's quote in the paragraph
○ Go over the answers with the class.

ANSWER KEY

These pictures of two families show a contrast in the way people lived in nineteenth-century America. Both families ~~was~~ were large ∧ but the similarity ends there. One picture tells us that some people ~~was~~ were wealthy and lived in great comfort. This family lived in a large house with art, expensive carpets, and long drapes that covered high windows. Their clothing was beautiful and clean. The children had toys to play with. Apparently, education was important; several family members are reading in this picture. In contrast ∧ the other picture tells us that some people were very poor. This family live∧d in a small, dark apartment with laundry hanging on the stove to dry. Their clothing was shabby and not very clean. There ~~isn't~~ aren't ∧ any toys or books in the photo. The life of these working-class people was probably very difficult, especially in a country of such wealth. ∧ As Du Bois said, " To be a poor man is hard, but to be a poor race in a land of dollars is the very bottom of hardships. " ∧

PART ⑤ ACADEMIC WRITING, PAGES 169–170

Writing Assignment

○ Go over the writing assignment. Make sure students see the possible topic sentences.
○ Have students read the five steps.
○ Direct students' attention to Step A, and have students choose one pair of pictures to write about. Remind students to use one of the topic sentences in the writing assignment box as a starting place.
○ Direct students' attention to Step B. Have students follow the steps.

WRITING STRATEGY: Writing a Paragraph of Comparison

○ Go over the information in the box.
○ Ask comprehension questions such as: *What do you write about in a paragraph of comparison? How should you organize your writing when you write about the differences between two things?*
○ Direct students' attention to the example. Give students time to read the example paragraph. Ask: *What is the writer's main idea? What support does the writer give for the idea that some families were wealthy? What is the main difference between the two families? What supporting details does the writer give for the idea that some families were very poor? What quote does the writer include? Why?*

○ Direct students' attention to Step C. Have students write paragraphs, using their notes from Step B. Remind students to use one of the topic sentences on page 169 and a quote from Part 1.
○ Direct students' attention to Step D. Have students read and edit their paragraphs, using the questions as a guideline.
○ To encourage peer editing, have students exchange paragraphs with a partner, edit, and return to the writer.
○ Direct students' attention to Step E. Have students rewrite the paragraphs.
○ Collect the paragraphs.

TOEFL® iBT Tip

TOEFL iBT Tip 6: The integrated writing skills on the TOEFL iBT requires students to think critically about material that they have read, interpret that information and relate it to a lecture, then present ideas in essay format.

○ Point out that the *Writing a Paragraph of Comparison* strategy and assignment corresponds to a strategy they will need to use when writing their independent essays. They will often be given two ideas and asked to argue for or against one of those ideas, or state a personal preference.

○ Remind students that they should leave themselves time to read over their work and edit for mistakes, particularly if they choose to type the essay on the computer.

EXPANSION ACTIVITY: Editing Practice

Photocopy and distribute the Black Line Master *Editing Practice* on page BLM 11.

○ Go over the directions.
○ Have students correct the mistakes and then compare answers with a partner.
○ Go over the answers with the class.

ANSWER KEY

There ~~was~~ _were_ a lot of changes in the United States in the 19th century. Many people move _d_ westward after the railroad was finished. Some ~~become~~ _became_ miners , but others were ranchers or farmers. Life ~~is~~ _was_ hard in the part of the country known as the Great Plains. Summers were hot and often without rain. In contrast , winters could be very cold and snowy. Life ~~weren't~~ _wasn't_ easy for the Native Americans. The new people ~~take~~ _took_ land from the Native Americans, forcing them to live on reservations. The second half of the 19th century ~~were~~ _was_ also a time of immigration. However , the immigrants were not only from Western Europe. Immigrants ~~come~~ _came_ from China, Italy, Russia, and Poland. In contrast to the earlier immigrants , the new immigrants ~~keep~~ _kept_ their own dress and customs, and they live _d_ in their own neighborhoods.

Unit 3 Vocabulary Workshop

○ Have students review vocabulary that they learned in Chapters 5 and 6.

A. Matching
○ Go over the directions.
○ Have students write the correct letters on the lines to match the definitions to the words
○ Go over the answers.

ANSWER KEY

1. h; 2. a; 3. i; 4. e; 5. f; 6. b; 7. j; 8. g; 9. d; 10. c

B. True or False?
○ Go over the directions.
○ Have students fill in the correct bubbles.
○ Go over the answers.

ANSWER KEY

1. T; 2. T; 3. F; 4. F; 5. T; 6. F; 7. T; 8. F

C. Words in Phrases
○ Go over the directions.
○ Have students write the words and phrases from the box on the lines to complete the phrases.
○ Go over the answers.

ANSWER KEY

1. business; 2. their religion; 3. beliefs; 4. town; 5. house; 6. drive; 7. a law

D. High Frequency Words
○ Go over the directions.
○ Have students fill in the blanks with words from the box.
○ Have students check their answers in the reading on pages 126–127.
○ Go over the answers.

ANSWER KEY

1. colonial; 2. exceptions; 3. popular; 4. both; 5. born; 6. taught; 7. unusual; 8. history; 9. first; 10. thirteen

Name: _____ **Date:** _____

Career Research

Directions: Complete the graphic organizer below to take notes on the career you researched.

Job title:	
Description of job tasks:	
Qualifications:	
Education/major that would be helpful in this job:	
Qualities of the job that make it attractive to me:	
Qualities of the job that make it unattractive or difficult for me:	

Editing Practice

Directions: There are 10 mistakes in punctuation, tenses, gerunds and infinitives, in the paragraph below. Find and correct them.

My ideal career is being a medical illustrator. this job is ideal for me because it matches my skills, interests, and values. When I was in college, I major in biology and art I have always love drawing pictures. I also enjoy to learn about the human body. I even considered to go into medicine. When I graduated, I decided going into medical illustration. I studied illustration since 2002, so I really understood the job now. I have has great practice in my classes, so I expect to get a job soon.

Graphic Organizer Practice

Directions: Complete the graphic organizer below to show important details for each idea.

Characteristics of the free enterprise system	

Laws determining price	

Problems with supply	

Name: _____   **Date:** _____

Editing Practice

Directions: There are 10 mistakes in stative verbs, tenses, prepositions of place, the order of adjectives, and spelling in the paragraph below. Find and correct them.

    Parents are the target about this VISA ad. On this ad, three Hispanic young children are playing in the yard. All three are seeming happy. One girl is having a water hose in her hand, and she is spraying water at the other two. She spraying an open mailbox. Behind the children is a white large house. The slogan Kids: Another reason to pay bills automatically with your VISA card" is above to their heads. There's information at the bottom the ad.

Compare and Contrast

Directions: Use the diagram to compare two classes of animals (for example, *insects* and *birds*). Write characteristics of one group (for example, *insects*) in the circle on the left, characteristics that group shares with the other group in the middle circle, and characteristics of the other group (for example, *birds*) in the circle on the right.

Group 1: _____   **Both groups**   **Group 2:** _____

Finding Examples

Directions: Complete the graphic organizer below to show examples for each place from the reading *Eating Bugs is Only Natural.*

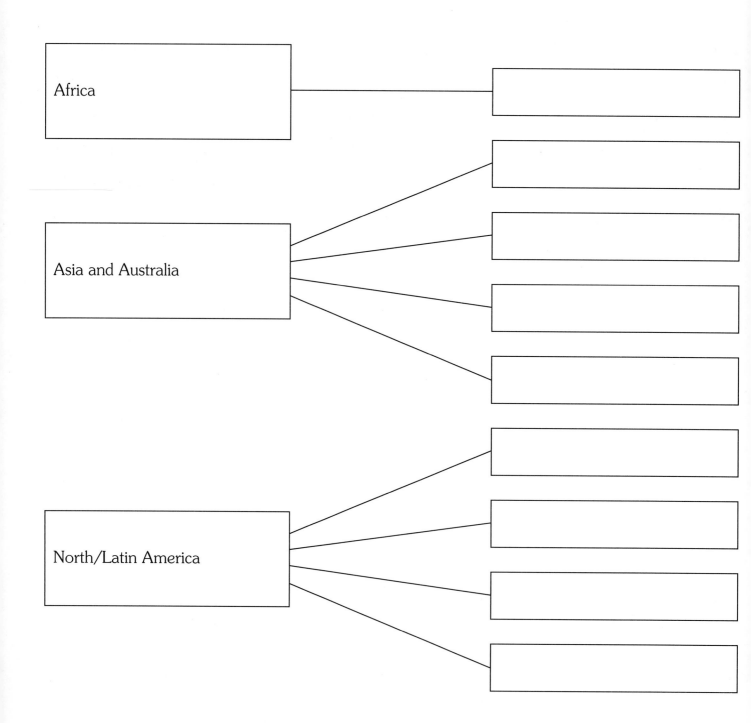

Editing Practice

Directions: There are 10 mistakes in count and noncount nouns, quantity expressions, and cause and effect statements. Find and correct them.

Linda has a healthy diet, but she could improve it. Her diet is healthy because she eats lot of fruits and vegetable. Fruits and vegetables have a vitamins. If you get a lot of vitamins, you won't be healthy. Linda doesn't eat too many butter or other fatty foods. If you eat too many fat, you will gain weight. Linda is a vegetarian, so she doesn't eat any meat. Meat is good source of protein. If you don't get too much protein, you might have health problems. Linda needs to eat more protein. She can eat nut or bean to get more protein.

The Name Game

Directions: Match the English last name to the profession or characteristic. Write the correct letter on the line.

ENGLISH LAST NAME

1. Archer _____
2. Armstrong _____
3. Baker _____
4. Brown _____
5. Carter _____
6. Carver _____
7. Chandler _____
8. Cook _____
9. Cooper _____
10. Duguid _____
11. Gardner _____
12. Hooper _____
13. Mayor _____
14. Miller _____
15. Naylor _____
16. Sawyer _____
17. Swift _____
18. Taylor _____
19. Turnbull _____
20. Walker _____

PROFESSION OR CHARACTERISTIC

a. someone who makes barrels
b. someone who moves very quickly
c. a man as strong as a bull
d. someone who does good and helps others
e. someone who makes clothes
f. a person who bakes bread
g. a person who grinds wheat in a mill
h. a person who saws wood
i. someone who walks around to inspect places
j. a person who puts hoops on barrels
k. someone who was the head of a village or town
l. someone who cooks
m. a person who makes nails
n. someone who carves wood
o. someone with brown hair
p. someone with strong arms
q. someone who works in a garden
r. a person who makes candles
s. a person who uses carts to transport goods
t. someone who hunts with a bow and arrow

Editing Practice

Directions: There are 10 mistakes in the simple past, *can* and *could,* and *force* and *make.* Find and correct them.

Many poor people in England come to the colonies as indentured servants. Unemployment were high, and they can't work in Great Britain. They signed a contract in England and agree to work for a period of four to seven years. In exchange, they receive their trip over for free and clothes, food, and shelter in the New World. However, the indentured servants were surprised at their new lives. Their masters often forced them work in the fields, instead of in their former professions. These servants cannot marry or have children. Their masters can sell their contract to someone else. The masters often maked the servants to live in poor conditions. Many died before they got their freedom.

Understanding Cause and Effect

1. **Directions:** Complete the graphic organizer below to show a cause and effect chain for changes in the western United States during the 19th century. Note that this is a simplified chain, and that there may be other causes and effects.

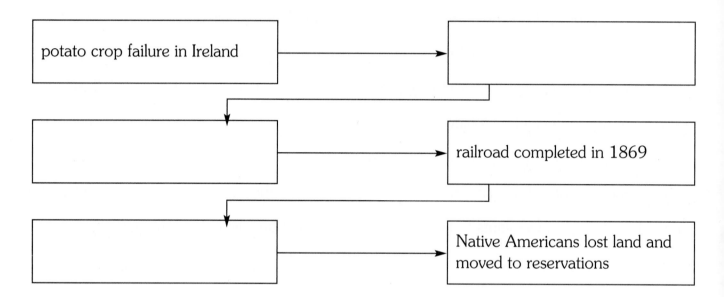

2. **Directions:** Complete the graphic organizer below to show a cause and effect chain to explain the rise of hostility towards immigrants in the United States.

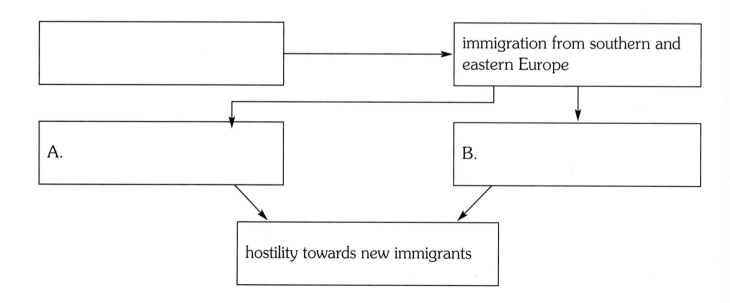

Editing Practice

Directions: There are 14 mistakes in punctuation, the use of *there,* the simple past tense, and the use of quotations. Find and correct them.

There was a lot of changes in the United States in the 19th century. Many people move westward after the railroad was finished. Some become miners but others were ranchers or farmers. Life is hard in the part of the country known as the Great Plains. Summers were hot and often without rain. In contrast winters could be very cold and snowy. Life weren't easy for the Native Americans. The new people take land from the Native Americans, forcing them to live on reservations. The second half of the 19th century were also a time of immigration. However the immigrants were not only from Western Europe. Immigrants come from China, Italy, Russia, and Poland. In contrast to the earlier immigrants the new immigrants keep their own dress and customs, and they live in their own neighborhoods.

Name _____ **Date** _____ **Score** _____

○ Reading

Directions: Read the paragraph below and fill in the correct answer for each of the questions that follow.

Frances Hawthorne works as an art therapist. Frances studied art and art history in college, and then went to graduate school to study visual arts. Although she always loved art, Frances also enjoyed helping people, especially children. She decided to go back to school and get a Master's degree in psychology. Now she uses a combination of art and psychology to help children and teenagers with their problems. When Frances meets with kids, they draw, paint, and work with clay. The art is good therapy because it helps them to express their feelings. Art therapy allows Frances to use both her skills and interests in art and psychology every day. Frances has found the perfect job.

1. What is the main idea of this passage?
    - Ⓐ Art therapy can help people.
    - Ⓑ Francis has found a job that uses her skills and interests.
    - Ⓒ Frances works with children.
    - Ⓓ Art therapy involves drawing and psychology.

2. What are Frances' qualifications for this job?
    - Ⓐ She has studied art and psychology.
    - Ⓑ She is a good artist.
    - Ⓒ She knows a lot about art history.
    - Ⓓ She has three children.

3. Why is art a good form of therapy, according to the reading?
    - Ⓐ It is quiet.
    - Ⓑ It is creative.
    - Ⓒ It helps people express their feelings.
    - Ⓓ It teaches people new skills.

4. What do you think is the best meaning of the expression "work with clay"?
    - Ⓐ draw
    - Ⓑ paint
    - Ⓒ another type of art
    - Ⓓ express problems

5. If someone likes to help people and is interested in how their minds work, what major should they choose?

- Ⓐ psychology
- Ⓑ art
- Ⓒ art history
- Ⓓ business

○ Strategy: Words in Phrases with Prepositions

Directions: For each sentence below, fill in the bubble to identify the correct preposition.

6. Frances was good _____ art and helping people.

| Ⓐ at | Ⓑ in | Ⓒ about | Ⓓ to |

7. She thought _____ working in a museum, but decided against it.

| Ⓐ at | Ⓑ in | Ⓒ about | Ⓓ to |

8. Values are the things you believe _____.

| Ⓐ at | Ⓑ in | Ⓒ about | Ⓓ to |

9. I've always been interested _____ medicine, but it takes so long to become a doctor.

| Ⓐ at | Ⓑ in | Ⓒ about | Ⓓ to |

10. Tom finally chose a job in finance, which was not related _____ his biology major.

| Ⓐ at | Ⓑ in | Ⓒ about | Ⓓ to |

○ Vocabulary

Directions: Fill in the bubble for the word or phrase that best completes each sentence.

11. If you like art and medicine, you might want to be a medical _____.

- Ⓐ doctor
- Ⓑ therapist
- Ⓒ illustrator

12. I don't want to be _____ a bad job forever.

- Ⓐ stuck in
- Ⓑ related to
- Ⓒ good at

13. Henry is a(n) _____ for a children's cartoon program.

- Ⓐ therapist
- Ⓑ animator
- Ⓒ scientist

14. Marta majored in communications and wants to become a _____.

- Ⓐ news anchor
- Ⓑ medical illustrator
- Ⓒ chef

15. A lot of college students think their parents should agree with their choice of career, but that is just a _____.

- Ⓐ facility
- Ⓑ myth
- Ⓒ major

16. Laura is a great accountant. She's really _____ math.

        Ⓐ related to   Ⓑ stuck in   Ⓒ good at

17. We're going to the art gallery because we're _____ that artist.

        Ⓐ stuck in   Ⓑ interested in   Ⓒ lead to

18. When you ask questions to learn about yourself, you are doing a _____.

        Ⓐ self-assessment   Ⓑ lifestyle   Ⓒ major

19. In looking at your _____, I can see you might be interested in medical illustration.

        Ⓐ facilities   Ⓑ profile   Ⓒ myth

20. Before Bill looks for a perfect job, he needs to know what his _____ are.

        Ⓐ values   Ⓑ myths   Ⓒ majors

◯ Mechanics

Directions: Complete the paragraph below with the correct form of the verb in parentheses. Use the simple present, simple past, present perfect, gerunds, or infinitives.

Julie _____ (be) a university student now. She _____ (attend) this
       21   **22**

school for three years. When she first _____ (start) college, Julie _____ (think)
                          23   **24**

about _____ (major) in business, because she really _____ (enjoy) math and
       25   **26**

_____ (work) with numbers. However, since last summer, Julie _____ (find) a
 27   **28**

volunteer job at the hospital. She _____ (love) the medical environment. Now, Julie wants
                          29

_____ (go) into hospital administration.
 30

◯ Editing

Directions: Find and correct the five mistakes in tenses, gerunds, and infinitives.

The best career for me is music therapy. I play a musical instrument for 15 years. I also study

music theory when I was in college. I even considered to become a musician. However, I'm really

interested in to help others, so I majored in psychology. Music therapy is a combination of my two

loves, so I decided to being a music therapist.

Name _____ Date _____ Score _____

○ Reading

Directions: Read the paragraph and sentences below. Fill in the bubble after each sentence to say if it is true or false.

Tweens, those between the ages of 8 and 14, are becoming an important market for advertisers. Kids at this age want to be like teenagers and not to be treated like young children. However, if an ad is at too high a level, the tweens won't understand it—it goes right over their heads. Another problem with marketing to tweens as if they are teens is that a lot of the advertising and products are just too mature. Many parents feel that their tweens are not ready for those products.

1. The main idea of the reading is: Advertisers don't know how to market to tweens.   ⓣ   ⓕ

2. Tweens respond most to advertising that is targeted toward children.   ⓣ   ⓕ

3. It "goes right over their heads" probably means that the idea presented is at too low a level.   ⓣ   ⓕ

4. Parents are worried that some ads and products are more appropriate for older teens.   ⓣ   ⓕ

5. Tweens would rather seem older than younger.   ⓣ   ⓕ

○ Strategy: Making Inferences

Directions: For each sentence below, fill in the bubble next to the best inference that follows.

6. The ad appeals to people who like to take cruises or other expensive vacations.
  - Ⓐ The advertisers want to attract the wealthy.
  - Ⓑ The focus of the ad campaign is on young people.
  - Ⓒ This ad is for vacation clothing.

7. Almost all of the orange trees were lost in the hurricane, so the price of orange juice went up.
  - Ⓐ The hurricane caused a billion dollars in damage.
  - Ⓑ Demand was greater than supply.
  - Ⓒ The growers were upset about the loss.

8. That brand of shoes had millions of pairs sold last year.

    Ⓐ The shoes were expensive.

    Ⓑ A lot of people bought the shoes.

    Ⓒ The line of shoes was developed last year.

9. The ads for that product appear on shows with mostly African-American actors.

    Ⓐ African Americans buy more products than other minorities.

    Ⓑ It is less expensive to advertise on TV shows that feature minorities.

    Ⓒ The advertisers want to attract African-American consumers.

10. In the old Soviet Union, the society did not have a free enterprise system.

    Ⓐ The government, not individuals and companies, owned the businesses.

    Ⓑ Russia does have a free enterprise system.

    Ⓒ In the Soviet system, prices never changed.

○ Vocabulary

Directions: Complete each sentence with a word from the box.

appeal to	frequent	retirement	trend
consumers	minority	shortage	
determine	motivations	surplus	

11. The destruction of oil wells in the oil-producing countries caused a _____ in oil around the world.

12. Only a _____ of students wanted the test tomorrow, so it's going to be Friday instead.

13. Most _____ want to pay a low price for a product.

14. There was a _____ of radios, so the store had a sale.

15. Everyone wants shoes like that. It's the latest _____.

16. That company doesn't sell a lot yet to young people. The advertisers would like the new ads

to _____ teenagers specifically.

17. Why do people buy what they do? It's those _____ that interest advertisers.

18. I sell sports equipment, so I want to attract people who _____ gyms and play on sports teams.

19. Some people volunteer in their _____. They miss the work and having a place to go every day.

20. How hard you study will _____ how well you do on the test.

○ Mechanics

Directions: Complete the sentences below with the correct form of the verb in parentheses. Use the simple present or the present continuous.

21. I can't talk right now. I _____ (have) lunch.

22. She _____ (look) sad. Her mother died last week.

23. The instructor _____ (think) I'm a bad student. I have to study more.

24. You _____ (remember) him, don't you?

25. He _____ (seem) upset.

26. I wonder what he _____ (think) about.

27. They _____ (want) to leave right now.

28. In the photo, a man _____ (walk) in a garden.

29. Which of you _____ (own) the white car outside?

30. What's the name of the magazine she _____ (look) at over there?

○ Editing

Directions: Find and correct the five mistakes in tense, prepositions, stative verbs, and order of adjectives.

Middle-aged women are the targets about this skin cream ad. In this ad, a very middle-aged attractive woman is looking at the camera. She is having brown beautiful hair and glowing skin. She is seeming happy. She looks young and confident.

Name _____ **Date** _____ **Score** _____

○ Reading

Directions: Read the paragraph below and fill in the correct answer for each of the questions that follow.

    The Gorilla Language Project studies how gorillas acquire language skills. The project has focused on teaching American Sign Language (ASL) to two gorillas, a female gorilla named Koko and a male gorilla named Michael. At the age of one, Koko became part of the project in 1971. Koko has learned to use more than 1,000 words in ASL, and to understand more than 2,000 words of spoken English. At the time of his death, Michael had a working vocabulary of more than 600 words. Both animals were able to invent new signs, tell stories, and make up jokes. The project has helped people understand how humans might have developed language long ago.

1. What is the main idea of this passage?
   - (A) Michael and Koko can speak ASL.
   - (B) Gorillas can use language like humans do.
   - (C) The Gorilla Language Project studies gorilla language skills.

2. Which gorilla has better language skills?
   - (A) Koko
   - (B) Michael
   - (C) Both gorillas are about the same.

3. How do the animals communicate?
   - (A) through gestures
   - (B) by saying words
   - (C) by a combination of spoken words and gestures

4. How can this research help us learn about human speech?
   - (A) We can learn new words from the gorillas.
   - (B) The research suggests how we might have learned to communicate in the past.
   - (C) We can see that gestures are more important than spoken words.

5. Which of the following statements is true based on the reading?
   - (A) Gorillas can learn language as well as humans.
   - (B) Gorillas can use language in a creative and funny way.
   - (C) Gorillas can copy human communication skills, but they can't create their own.

○ Strategy: Understanding Punctuation

Directions: For each sentence below, fill in the bubble to identify the reason for the quotation marks or italics.

6. The ducks followed their "mother," the caretaker at the duck pond.
   - Ⓐ to state a person's exact words
   - Ⓑ the word really means something different
   - Ⓒ a title

7. When she heard, "Ready or not, here I come," she hid.
   - Ⓐ to state a person's exact words
   - Ⓑ for emphasis
   - Ⓒ the words really mean something different

8. I read the *New York Times* every day.
   - Ⓐ for emphasis
   - Ⓑ to mean "the word"
   - Ⓒ a title

9. That's the *last* place he would want to go tonight.
   - Ⓐ for emphasis
   - Ⓑ to mean "the word"
   - Ⓒ the word really means something different

10. *School* is a group of fish.
    - Ⓐ a title
    - Ⓑ to mean "the word"
    - Ⓒ for stress

○ Vocabulary

Directions: Fill in the bubble for the word or phrase that best completes each sentence.

11. Dolphins that are raised in _____ live longer than dolphins that have been raised by humans.
    - Ⓐ the wild
    - Ⓑ captivity
    - Ⓒ territoriality

12. An animal that is _____ survives better than animals that can't change in a new environment.
    - Ⓐ distinct
    - Ⓑ wild
    - Ⓒ adaptable

13. One animal that is similar to man is the _____.
    - Ⓐ cub
    - Ⓑ ape
    - Ⓒ jackdaw

14. When animals move from one area to another with the seasons, it's called _____.
    - Ⓐ habituation
    - Ⓑ imprinting
    - Ⓒ migration

15. Some birds learn to recognize other members of their species through _____.
    - Ⓐ habituation
    - Ⓑ insight
    - Ⓒ imprinting

16. Humans are not the only animal that can use _____ to solve problems.
    - Ⓐ insight
    - Ⓑ imprinting
    - Ⓒ conditioning

17. I didn't mean to jump—it was just _____.
    - Ⓐ a reflex
    - Ⓑ insight
    - Ⓒ a gesture

18. _____ are a form of communication that can mean different things to different cultures.
    - Ⓐ Instincts
    - Ⓑ Gestures
    - Ⓒ Reflexes

19. Her use of vocabulary is really advanced, but her _____ is not as good.

     Ⓐ call   Ⓑ instinct   Ⓒ syntax

20. My dog likes to _____ a ball when I throw it.

     Ⓐ prey on   Ⓑ salivate   Ⓒ fetch

○ Mechanics

Directions: Complete the paragraph below by selecting the correct word in parentheses.

I used to watch a TV show _____ (when/because) I was young. It was about

_____ (a/the) dolphin. _____ (A/The) dolphin lived with _____ (a/the) family of a
22   23   24

father and two sons. _____ (A/The) younger boy _____ (swimmed/swam) with
25   26

the dolphin and _____ (called/caught) him Flipper. They spent a lot of time together
27

_____ (when/because) they were friends. _____ (A/The) boy and Flipper could
28   29

even _____ (talk/"talk") with each other, although they didn't actually speak.
30

○ Editing

Directions: Find and correct the five mistakes with the simple past tense, direct and indirect objects, transition words, and punctuation.

About ten years ago, the researcher went to Africa to studied elephants. The researcher wanted

to see if elephants could learn to play musical instruments. First, he gave to the elephants drums

and harmonicas. Next he taught the elephants how to play. One thing surprised the researcher. He

didn't expected the elephants to play after he left at the end of the day. The elephants' "music"

woke him up.

Name _____ **Date** _____ **Score** _____

○ Reading

Directions: Read the paragraph and sentences below. Fill in the bubble after each sentence to say if it is true or false.

Many people who want to lose weight go on a diet high in protein and low in carbohydrates. Protein sources such as beef, fish, chicken, and beans stay in your stomach longer and so allow you to feel full for a longer time. Proteins are also broken down more slowly and supply energy more steadily. Not all proteins are equally healthy however. Nuts and some kinds of fish supply a type of fatty acid that keeps your heart healthy. In contrast, red meat contains a lot of an unhealthy type of fat known as saturated fat. Most nutritionists—people who work in the field of nutrition— recommend eating more of the healthy sources of protein (fish, chicken, beans and nuts) and less of the unhealthy sources (red meat and whole milk), if you want to maintain a good weight and good health.

1. The main idea of the reading is: Some proteins have saturated fat. ⓣ ⓕ

2. Eating a high protein diet will make someone lose weight. ⓣ ⓕ

3. You may not get as hungry if you eat a diet high in protein. ⓣ ⓕ

4. Nutritionists are medical doctors. ⓣ ⓕ

5. Some sources of protein, such as beef and whole milk, are healthier than others. ⓣ ⓕ

○ Strategy: Using Figures and Tables

Directions: For each question below, fill in the bubble next to the best answer. Use the information in the chart.

TABLE 4.1 VITAMINS

Vitamin	How Used in Body	Problems if Not Enough	Foods	RDA
A (retinol)	vision, healthy skin	night blindness, rough skin	liver, broccoli, carrots	5000 IU
B1 (thiamine)	allows cells to use carbohydrates	digestive problems, muscle paralysis	ham, eggs, raisins	1.5 mg
B2 (riboflavin)	allows cells to use carbohydrates and proteins	eye problems, cracking skin	milk, yeast, eggs	1.7 mg
B3 (niacin)	allows cells to carry out respiration	mental problems, skin rash, diarrhea	peanuts, tuna, chicken	20.0 mg

6. Which vitamin is found in peanuts?

        Ⓐ retinol   Ⓑ thiamine   Ⓒ riboflavin   Ⓓ niacin

7. Which food is a source of retinol?

        Ⓐ broccoli   Ⓑ eggs   Ⓒ milk   Ⓓ tuna

8. How many milligrams of B2 should you get each day?

        Ⓐ 5000   Ⓑ 1.5   Ⓒ 1.7   Ⓓ 20.0

9. What can cause night blindness?

        Ⓐ too much retinol   Ⓒ too much thiamine

        Ⓑ not enough retinol   Ⓓ not enough thiamine

10. If you don't get enough riboflavin, what may happen?

        Ⓐ muscle paralysis   Ⓒ diarrhea

        Ⓑ cracking skin   Ⓓ mental problems

○ Vocabulary

Directions: Complete each sentence with a word from the box.

aquatic	entomology	nutrients	protein	taboo
carbohydrates	fats	pesticides	retinol	tradition

11. Fish are _____ animals.

12. Some farmers don't like to use _____, so they find other ways to prevent insect damage to their crops.

13. Some foods are _____ in other cultures. For example, Hindus will not eat beef because cows are sacred.

14. In the Atkins diet, fats and proteins are allowed, but _____ are not.

15. In my family, it is a _____ to have roast beef on New Year's Day.

16. Fish, nuts, and meat are good sources of _____.

17. Oil and butter are examples of _____.

18. _____ are chemicals in food and include proteins, fats, carbohydrates, vitamins, minerals, and water.

19. _____ is another name for Vitamin A.

20. _____ is the study of insects.

○ Mechanics

Directions: Complete the sentences below with the correct word or phrase in parentheses.

21. Can you buy _____ (a bread/bread) there?

22. Mutton _____ (is/are) a good substitute for pork in Muslim countries.

23. He drank _____ (too much/too many) cups of coffee yesterday.

24. She didn't have _____ (a lot of/enough) water, so she fainted.

25. We need _____ (some/a) milk, don't we?

26. Americans probably eat _____ (too much/too many) red meat.

27. Americans probably don't eat _____ (enough/too many) fruit.

28. If you don't get enough vitamins, you _____ (will/won't) get sick.

29. Orange juice has a lot of _____ (vitamin C/vitamin Cs).

30. Not enough protein in a diet _____ (cause/causes) health problems.

○ Editing

Directions: Find and correct the five mistakes in count and noncount nouns, quantity expressions, and cause/effect statements.

Why are people interested in a Mediterranean food? Recent research suggests that if you eat the traditional food of Mediterranean countries (for example, Italy), you were healthy. People there eat a lot of olive oils but not too many butter. They eat fresh vegetables, fish, and whole grains. However, it may not be just the food that makes people healthy. They also get many exercise.

Name _____ **Date** _____ **Score** _____

◯ Reading

Directions: Read the paragraph below and fill in the correct answer for each of the questions that follow.

From the 15th century until the 19th century, slaves were traded in a triangular trade route. The first part of this three-part route was the passage from England to Africa. Many African tribes had slaves and were willing to trade slaves for European goods. English ships brought trinkets, guns, and alcohol to exchange for African slaves. On the middle part of the route, the ships carried the slaves to the Americas to provide a work force for the colonies. There was a high mortality rate on this part of the trip. Many Africans died because of hardships such as poor treatment and malnutrition. They were fed very little food, and it wasn't fresh. The slaves stayed down below in the cargo area. This area usually held goods and supplies. When the ships reached the Americas, the slaves were sold to work on plantations. Cotton, sugar, and tobacco were grown on these large farms. In the last part of the route, the ships then carried tobacco, cotton, sugar, and rum from the colonies back to England and other countries in Europe.

1. What is the main idea of the reading?
   - Ⓐ Many slaves died on the trip from Africa.
   - Ⓑ The slave trade was part of a larger trade system between three continents.
   - Ⓒ Africans liked receiving guns in exchange for providing slaves.
2. What did Africans receive in trade from Europe?
   - Ⓐ guns   Ⓑ slaves   Ⓒ sugar
3. What did England receive through the triangular trade?
   - Ⓐ guns   Ⓑ slaves   Ⓒ sugar
4. According to the reading, why were Africans taken to the Americas?
   - Ⓐ to work on plantations   Ⓑ to hold cargo   Ⓒ to get European goods
5. In this reading, what do you think the word *passage* means?
   - Ⓐ a trip   Ⓑ a story   Ⓒ a door

◯ Strategy: Guessing the Meanings of New Words: Using an Explanation in the Next Sentence

Directions: For each sentence below, fill in the bubble next to the best definition for the word in bold. Refer to the reading.

6. What does **triangular** mean?
   - Ⓐ slave   Ⓑ having three sides   Ⓒ trade

7. What is a **mortality rate**?

     Ⓐ poor treatment   Ⓑ bad diet   Ⓒ the number of people who died

8. What is **malnutrition**?

     Ⓐ eating poor   Ⓑ receiving poor treatment   Ⓒ not getting enough
         quality food   fresh air

9. What do you think **cargo** is?

     Ⓐ slaves   Ⓑ goods and supplies   Ⓒ passenger rooms
                          that are traded

10. What do you think **plantations** are?

     Ⓐ large farms   Ⓑ large factories   Ⓒ ships

◯ Vocabulary

Directions: Fill in the bubble for the word or phrase that best completes each sentence.

11. After he _____, he had more time to relax.

     Ⓐ protested   Ⓑ retired   Ⓒ boycotted

12. Scientists often do research to test their _____.

     Ⓐ theories   Ⓑ grievances   Ⓒ exceptions

13. A small _____ published her book.

     Ⓐ repeal   Ⓑ trade   Ⓒ printing shop

14. The unhappy students gave a list of their _____ to the instructor.

     Ⓐ grievances   Ⓑ theories   Ⓒ writs of assistance

15. In the 1970s, Cesar Chavez led a _____ against grape growers. Many consumers didn't buy grapes for years.

     Ⓐ grievance   Ⓑ exception   Ⓒ boycott

16. The area soccer teams _____ to form one organization.

     Ⓐ boycotted   Ⓑ united   Ⓒ repealed

17. We _____ the unfair treatment, but no one listened.

     Ⓐ protested   Ⓑ traded   Ⓒ retired

18. Lisa wore white, but everyone else wore black. She was _____.

     Ⓐ a grievance   Ⓑ a patriot   Ⓒ an exception

19. Most countries cannot produce everything they need, so they _____ with others.

     Ⓐ trade   Ⓑ repeal   Ⓒ retire

20. The United States used to have a law that made drinking alcohol illegal, but the law was_____.

     Ⓐ united   Ⓑ traded   Ⓒ repealed

○ Mechanics

Directions: Complete the sentences below with one of the words or phrases in parentheses.

21. When I was a child, I _____ (can't/couldn't) swim very well.

22. Now I _____ (can/could) swim at least a mile.

23. The colonists were forced _____ (to pay/pay) taxes even though they were not represented in the British government.

24. Maria's mother made her _____ (to clean/clean) her room.

25. In Colonial America, women _____ (cannot/could not) vote.

26. In the United States, you _____ (cannot/could not) vote until you are 18 years old.

27. Many slave-owners _____ (forced/made) slaves to work very long hours under poor conditions.

28. John _____ (can/could) speak English very well, so he doesn't take classes anymore.

29. We _____ (can't/couldn't) hear the lecture, so we moved closer.

30. The British government passed laws that _____ (forced/made) the colonists shelter soldiers in their homes.

○ Editing

Directions: Find and correct the five mistakes with the simple past tense, *can* and *could, force* and *make.*

Colonial women didn't had the same rights we do today. They usually married very young, in their teens. Once they were married, they become the property of their husbands. They can't vote or be witnesses in court, and they couldn't control their own property or money. If they run away from their husbands, they could be arrested for stealing, because they took themselves and their clothing. In some places, people wanted to pass laws that would force widows—women whose husbands died—remarry within seven years!

Name _____ **Date** _____ **Score** _____

○ Reading

Directions: Read the paragraph and sentences below. Fill in the bubble after each sentence to say if it is true or false.

In the late 19th century, a group of businessmen became powerful. Some called them "robber barons," a term that described them in a negative way. These men were successful industrialists who expanded their businesses and became very wealthy. They used modern practices in their factories. Although men like Andrew Carnegie and John D. Rockefeller helped the economy in general by making their steel and oil businesses more productive, they were also criticized for not helping their workers. Many of their workers were very poor, received bad treatment in the factories, and lived in terrible conditions.

1. The main idea of the reading is: robber barons were wealthy.   Ⓣ   Ⓕ

2. The industrialists had only a positive effect on the country.   Ⓣ   Ⓕ

3. The reading only talks about the lives of the industrialists.   Ⓣ   Ⓕ

4. The reading describes how the factories became more modern.   Ⓣ   Ⓕ

5. According to the reading, the wealthy industrialists did not   Ⓣ   Ⓕ
do enough to help the workers.

○ Strategy: Finding Specific Support

Directions: Match each general sentence below with the correct specific support statement.

> **Specific Support**
> **a.** They lost their land, and many lost their lives to war and disease.
> **b.** Many people had guns, and others stole cattle or robbed the railroads.
> **c.** They helped complete the railroad.
> **d.** They faced drought, bad weather, and sometimes unfriendly Native Americans.
> **e.** Increased industrialization led to the rise of large successful companies like Carnegie Steel.

General Sentence

6. Irish immigrants contributed to westward expansion. _____

7. Native Americans suffered during the 19th century. _____

8. Homesteaders had a difficult life. _____

9. There was a lot of violence and crime in some western towns. _____

10. It was also a time of great economic development. _____

○ Vocabulary

Directions: Complete each sentence with a word from the box.

buffalo	hostility	reservations
cattle drives	miners	train track
drought	newcomers	
homesteaders	plains	

11. Many recent _____ to the United States are from Latin American countries.

12. _____ moved west because they could get free land to settle on.

13. The _____ moved west to search for gold and silver.

14. Most _____ are poor, and Indians have trouble making a living there.

15. During a _____ the land dries up, and it's hard for the crops to grow.

16. Immigrants sometimes face _____ in their new countries, especially if they seem to be taking jobs from the people who already live there.

17. The immigrants worked hard to build the _____ for the railroad company.

18. During the 19th and 20th centuries, ranchers brought their beef to market on long _____ .

19. Some ranchers are raising _____, because they have found, like the Native Americans did, that it is a good source of meat.

20. The _____ are broad flat areas of land.

○ Mechanics

Directions: Complete the sentences below by selecting the correct word or phrase in parentheses.

21. The United States is a big country, _____ (but/in contrast) it seemed smaller after the railroad was completed.

22. There _____ (were/was) a lot of land available to settlers after the Homestead Act was passed.

23. There _____ (were/was) many Native Americans living on reservations at the end of the 19th century.

24. How many immigrants _____ (were/was) there in New York City?

25. English immigrants could speak the language and adapt easily to the new country.

_____, (But/In contrast) Russian Jews kept their own language and lived in separate neighborhoods.

26. Many people _____ (come/came) to the U.S. in the 19th century to find a better life.

27. Immigrants still _____ (move/moved) to other countries looking for better jobs and better treatment.

28. There _____ (was/were) some hostility towards immigrants.

29. Chinese immigrants worked very hard on the railroad. _____, (But/However) the United States passed laws that said no more Chinese could come here.

30. Some of the people who _____ (went/gone) west became miners or ranchers.

○ Editing

Directions: Find and correct the five mistakes in simple past tense, the use of *there + be,* the use of quotations, and punctuation of transition words.

In the 19th century, there was frequent conflicts between ranchers and homesteaders. Homesteaders came out and claimed free government land for their farms. In contrast ranchers needed lots of land for their cattle. The ranchers were used to feeding and driving their cattle on the government land. Both sides start to fence large areas of land but this led to more problems. People started cutting the fences and fencing land that wasn't theirs. The cattle sometimes died when they got stuck at a fence. As one person said, I saw drifts of dead cattle along that fence sometimes 400 yards wide.

Chapter 1 Test Answer Key

Reading

1. B; 2. A; 3. C; 4. C; 5. A

Strategy: Words in Phrases with Prepositions

6. A; 7. C; 8. B; 9. B; 10. D

Vocabulary

11. C; 12. A; 13. B; 14. A; 15. B; 16. C; 17. B; 18. A; 19. B; 20. A

Mechanics

21. is; 22. has attended; 23. started; 24. thought; 25. majoring; 26. enjoys/enjoyed; 27. working; 28. has found; 29. loves; 30. to go

Editing

The best career for me is music therapy. I ~~play~~ _{have played} a musical instrument for 15 years. I also ~~study~~ _{studied} music theory when I was in college. I even considered ~~to become~~ _{becoming} a musician. However, I'm really interested in ~~to help~~ _{helping} others, so I majored in psychology. Music therapy is a combination of my two loves, so I decided to be~~ing~~ a music therapist.

Chapter 2 Test Answer Key

Reading

1. F; 2. F; 3. F; 4. T; 5. T

Strategy: Making Inferences

6. A; 7. B; 8. B; 9. C; 10. A

Vocabulary

11. shortage; 12. minority; 13. consumers; 14. surplus; 15. trend; 16. appeal to; 17. motivations; 18. frequent; 19. retirement; 20. determine

Mechanics

21. am having; 22. looks; 23. thinks; 24. remember; 25. seems; 26. is thinking; 27. want; 28. is walking; 29. owns; 30. is looking

Editing

Middle-aged women are the targets ~~about~~ _{for} this skin cream ad. In this ad, a very ~~middle-aged attractive~~ _{attractive middle-aged} woman is looking at the camera. She ~~is having~~ _{has} ~~brown beautiful~~ _{beautiful brown} hair and glowing skin. She ~~is seeming~~ _{seems} happy. She looks young and confident.

Chapter 3 Test Answer Key

Reading

1. C; 2. A; 3. A; 4. B; 5. B

Strategy: Understanding Punctuation

6. B; 7. A; 8. C; 9. A; 10. B

Vocabulary

11. A; 12. C; 13. B; 14. C; 15. C; 16. A; 17. A; 18. B; 19. C; 20. C

Mechanics

21. when; 22. a; 23. The; 24. a; 25. The; 26. swam; 27. called; 28. because; 29. The; 30. "talk"

Editing

About ten years ago, ~~the~~ ^a⋀ researcher went to Africa to ~~studied~~ ^{study}⋀ elephants. The researcher wanted to see if elephants could learn to play musical instruments. First, he gave ~~to~~ the elephants drums and harmonicas. Next ⋀_, he taught the elephants how to play. One thing surprised the researcher. He didn't expect~~ed~~ the elephants to play after he left at the end of the day. The elephants' "music" woke him up.

Chapter 4 Test Answer Key

Reading

1. F; 2. F; 3. T; 4. F; 5. F

Strategy: Using Figures and Tables

6. D; 7. A; 8. C; 9. B; 10. B

Vocabulary

11. aquatic; 12. pesticides; 13. taboo; 14. carbohydrates; 15. tradition; 16. protein; 17. fats; 18. Nutrients; 19. Retinol; 20. Entomology

Mechanics

21. bread; 22. is; 23. too many; 24. enough; 25. some; 26. too much; 27. enough; 28. will; 29. vitamin C; 30. causes

Editing

Why are people interested in ~~a~~ Mediterranean food? Recent research suggests that if you eat the traditional food of Mediterranean countries (for example, Italy), you ~~were~~ ^{will be}⋀ healthy. People there eat a lot of olive oil~~s~~ but not too ~~many~~ ^{much}⋀ butter. They eat fresh vegetables, fish, and whole grains. However, it may not be just the food that makes people healthy. They also get ~~many~~ ^{a lot of}⋀ exercise.

Chapter 5 Test Answer Key

Reading

1. B; 2. A; 3. C; 4. A; 5. A

Strategy: Guessing the Meanings of New Words: Using an Explanation in the Next Sentence

6. B; 7. C; 8. A; 9. B; 10. A

Vocabulary

11. B; 12. A; 13. C; 14. A; 15. C; 16. B; 17. A; 18. C; 19. A; 20. C

Mechanics

21. couldn't; 22. can; 23. to pay; 24. clean; 25. could not; 26. cannot; 27. forced; 28. can; 29. couldn't; 30. made

Editing

Colonial women didn't ~~had~~ ^have^ the same rights we do today. They usually married very young, in their teens. Once they were married, they ~~become~~ ^became^ the property of their husbands. They ~~can't~~ ^couldn't^ vote or be witnesses in court, and they couldn't control their own property or money. If they ~~run~~ ^ran^ away from their husbands, they could be arrested for stealing, because they took themselves and their clothing. In some places, people wanted to pass laws that would force widows—women whose husbands died—^to^ remarry within seven years!

Chapter 6 Test Answer Key

Reading

1. F. 2. F; 3. F; 4. F; 5. T

Strategy: Finding Specific Support

6. c; 7. a; 8. d; 9. b; 10. e

Vocabulary

11. newcomers; 12. Homesteaders; 13. miners; 14. reservations; 15. drought; 16. hostility; 17. train track; 18. cattle drives; 19. buffalo; 20. plains

Mechanics

21. but; 22. was; 23. were; 24. were; 25. In contrast; 26. came; 27. move; 28. was; 29. However; 30. went

Editing

In the 19th century, there ~~was~~ ^were^ frequent conflicts between ranchers and homesteaders. Homesteaders came out and claimed free government land for their farms. In contrast ^,^ ranchers needed lots of land for their cattle. The ranchers were used to feeding and driving their cattle on the government land. Both sides start^ed^ to fence large areas of land ^,^ but this led to more problems. People started cutting the fences and fencing land that wasn't theirs. The cattle sometimes died when they got stuck at a fence. As one person said, ^"^I saw drifts of dead cattle along that fence sometimes 400 yards wide.^"^